Cp 50

storms
and illuminations

18 years of access theatre

storms
and illuminations

18 years of access theatre

by cynthia wisehart

foreword by michael douglas

introduction by anthony edwards

emily *publications*

Copyright © 1997 Cynthia Wisehart.

Published by Emily Publications.

2428 Chapala Street, Santa Barbara, California 93105.

All rights reserved.

Cover photograph © 1996 Jeff Brouws.

Back cover photograph © 1985 Michael Hughs.

Design by The Lily Guild Temple of Design, Santa Barbara.

Imagesetting by Tom Buhl Imaging Center.

Printed in the USA by Ventura Printing.

ISBN #0-9656894-0-9

Table of **contents**

to the Access Theatre family
for their stories, and

to my parents
who sewed, chauffeured, critiqued, and applauded.

In 1981, Rod Lathim invited me to a rehearsal for his second production *Through Our Eyes* and I went, a little reluctantly. I stayed for two hours. Watching the actors tell their own stories, there was a clarity and directness that was unsettling but impossible to resist, and an honesty I don't often see in theater.

One of my great joys has been bringing people to see the company perform, and to experience what I felt that first day. You can always sense the initial tension or awkwardness in the audience, and then the production just seduces them and they find themselves suddenly vulnerable and open, caught up in the experience and savoring the performance of the actors.

When I think of the company over these last eighteen years I see so many good shows, moments of humor and love and accomplishment that are included in this book. Rod has taken us all on a momentous ride really, as the company grew from a small community theater to reach international audiences and millions of people through television.

The members of Access Theatre achieved this producing original plays and musicals, which is remarkable in itself. They successfully and powerfully addressed a host of social issues, they enlightened and entertained, they built community. Above all, the key to Access Theatre's success was that it was great theater.

For me, what marks the productions is a feeling of watching something that has such truth to it that all else is forgotten and for a moment in time there is a bond between audience and performers. It can open people's minds to a broader acceptance of people with disabilities and the fact that artists with disabilities are legitimate artists.

But I think it also gives people an experience of humanity, their own and the actors'. It tears down boundaries. This gives the Access Theatre an immortality, because what happened on their stage on a single night reached beyond the performance, beyond the individuals, and out into the world.

Michael Douglas

Los Angeles, 1996

preface

I did the interviews for this book over a two-year period between 1994 and 1996, and during that time met more than one hundred people who had participated in Access Theatre. When I was almost finished with the book, the company's founder and artistic director, Rod Lathim, decided it was time to leave, and the board of directors chose to close Access Theatre. So this has become a memoir of sorts.

But I don't think this book is really about the past. And it's not really about disability. I think it's about theater, and the way striving to create something brings people to a common ground, and to personal revelations about themselves and others.

What struck me most about Access Theatre – in the stories I heard, the letters I read, the performances I saw – was the sheer power of the human voice in all it's various expressions, and the power of good it does people to be heard and to listen in new ways. Many people in the audience found that lifelong questions were addressed by actors with whom they thought they had nothing in common. Many people on

the stage were proud to be speaking the truth as they knew it. That is the nature of theater, or it can be.

During this process I caught myself in many little assumptions. For example, my naïve realization that all disabilities are not the same, that a person who uses a wheelchair may be intimidated by people who are deaf, that someone who is blind may not relate to a person with cerebral palsy, in short that disability is not automatically a unifier in some categorical sense.

What *is* unifying, for the brief time that a company works together on a show, or an audience sits in the dark and takes it in, is communication. Not the usual code with all its labels, rituals, and repetition, but the communication that happens when expectations are broken down, when new methods are tried – when you learn to recognize and discard a "hearing" joke in favor of one that everyone can appreciate; when you strain to understand someone who speaks with effort, yet chooses his words with economy and wit; when you dance with a cavalier in a wheelchair. People with disabilities found their Access Theatre experience liberating. Many, many non-disabled people did too, and realized to their deep personal relief that perfection and conformity are not prerequisites for participation in the human race.

The artists of Access Theatre counted on this: that if you put people in a room where they are free as one reviewer said "to stare" they will recognize and embrace an actor's humanity. They will see past the details such as wheelchairs and sign language, and see people without needing to be told. So Access Theatre was not radical by message, only by example. It was also an out-of-the-ordinary experience in a world where living with a disability is still misunderstood, expensive, hugely inconvenient, and for many a daily civil rights project.

The people I talked to for this book struggled for the best and most honest words to describe their experience of Access Theatre. When they said it was a family – as many did – they chose that description with care. So these photographs are an album of the last eighteen years. The stories are a few of many, a fraction of them I must assume. Some stories I've told only once, though I heard them from many people; some good stories I've left out because like the one about Solomon's scarf and the mud puddle, you really had to be there, as they say. I also thought it might be helpful to add chapters about how the company dealt with sign language, stagecraft, accessibility, and fundraising. This gave me a chance to acknowledge some of the many people who worked behind the scenes, and to illustrate some of what they accomplished.

I tried to include a range of people – there have been more than I've named, and everybody I've mentioned contributed more than I have shown. I tried to let them do the talking, because I wasn't there myself. I hope I've captured some of what they shared in the strange and affecting world of theater, because behind the wonderful stage pictures was a process as rich and imperfect as any human endeavor, as any family.

Cynthia Wisehart

December, 1996

introduction

I grew up in Santa Barbara, California and it was a lucky thing for an actor. The community was full of opportunities to perform, and my friends and I participated enthusiastically without knowing how unique the situation was. When Rod started Access Theatre, and began to write and produce his own shows, it didn't seem such an unusual thing. We were used to seeing grassroots theater companies in town; most of us already knew that theater needed to include original works, and not just revivals of *South Pacific* and *Hello, Dolly*! Though local actors were aware that Rod cast artists with disabilities, his company was most of all about making theater, and it seemed like everyone I knew wanted, very badly, to make theater.

By 1989, Access Theatre was inviting me home to speak at their 10th anniversary gala. They had by that time produced twelve original works, many I had seen. In 1990, I acted in the company's production of *The Boys Next Door*, a show that I enjoyed doing and I think did credit to Tom Griffin's wonderful play. But my most intimate association with the company was during *Storm Reading* for which I served as audience member, "celebrity supporter" and documentary filmmaker.

In fall of 1988, I traveled with the *Storm Reading* tour for two weeks in Colorado, New Mexico and Arizona. With my collaborators Shaun Hardin and Chick Cashman, I accumulated 22 hours of footage, which ultimately became a half-hour film, *Speaking Through Walls*.

We came up with the title over a meal with Neil Marcus, who co-wrote and acts in *Storm Reading*. Neil is famous for his table manners and for making people join in and eat with the same kind of recklessness he does. Neil's body does not do exactly what he'd like it to all the time; he's the kind of person many people turn away from. But Neil likes to use the opportunity, and he will urge people to imitate him, to dive into their fears and come out the other side – usually covered with spaghetti. The experience seemed at the time like breaking through a wall and finding a way to connect and communicate despite physical obstacles. Neil got us to joke and participate in life through the window of his disability, but he was also able to bring out his fears, frustrations, and insights. It's a potent combination, and *Storm Reading* became Access Theatre's most visible message to the world.

But this book is not just about one play – Access Theatre produced 24 productions over 18 years and these are the stories of those years. It is also the story of Rod Lathim. It is impossible to separate Access Theatre's history from its founder and artistic director. The company was pretty much his whole life for a long time, which was not always a good thing. He became a representative of something, a diplomat and a fundraiser, when I think at times he would have rather been just an artist.

In many ways, Access Theatre was Rod's very personal goal and vision. His ideas were not so much about disability issues, though the company addressed those issues and others. Most of all, Access Theatre created an environment that was a little more equal than most and tried to set an example for inclusion, which seems to be more important to Rod than revolution. In fact Rod is most comfortable very near the border of sentimentality. He was sometimes criticized for being too sentimental, I've said it myself. He was criticized for not being militant enough. Everyone's a critic. But disability was never the point of Access Theatre. The point was to focus on similarities, to blend experiences, and to break down barriers – to prove that an artist with a disability can collaborate with other artists, to prove that a unique artist like Neil Marcus can come from anywhere.

I can say from first hand experience, from the tentative overtures casting directors have made to me, from discussions that follow when people learn of my involvement with the company, that Access Theatre opened some doors of opportunity and some people's eyes. I think it will always be a struggle to be involved in theater, television, and films. It is difficult to get your voice heard and not be drowned out by the commercial realities and politics all artists face. It's hard not to feel a sense of us and them. But Access Theatre fought a very good fight to be heard, and to create a message that was both accessible and universal.

I remember someone pointing out to me that we are all born disabled, if we are lucky we will live to be disabled by old age, and we will face other disabilities along the way. For some the disabilities will be much harder and more painful. This is not news. Access Theatre reminded us that if the only part of our lives worth living is whatever time we can claim to be able-bodied and able-minded, then we are cheating ourselves out of our lives. And if we choose our friends, lovers, mentors and collaborators only from among the able-looking we lose again. Bodies are fragile, spirit is strong, and I got to experience that through my work with Neil Marcus and Access Theatre. I learned a few more things about communicating. I was excited to see that my chosen profession offers opportunity to shake up expectations, to share in a process that is sincere and a result that is resonant. Not everything Access Theatre produced achieved all this, but as you will see in this book, it gave a lot of people their own epiphanies large and small.

I think magic and imagination are as basic a need as water. Without a chance to contemplate the world through the creative experience it's so easy to fall prey to simplistic and judgmental answers to the confounding questions we face as humans. We can harden and give up. Access Theatre helped people in their quest for meaning and stamina in the human race. The company brought some people together who probably wouldn't have had occasion to speak to each other, much less know each other well. We all got to make a little art together, and I can't believe as I sit here now, it's 18 years gone by.

Anthony Edwards

Los Angeles, 1996

Michael Spencer, *Footlight Fantasy*, Lobero Theatre, 1981

One of the more popular Chinese proverbs says that "the journey of a thousand miles begins with a single step." For Access Theatre, a long and remarkable journey began – more accurately – with a sprint.

On May 10, 1979, *Circus of Life* had sold out the Lobero Theatre and the last stragglers collected their tickets at the box office. At five minutes before curtain, the esteemed director raced past them and down Canon Perdido Street in hot pursuit of four young boys; a full-blown case of stage fright had flowered into the obvious response – flight.

An hour later, and with the refugees tucked back into the fold, a company of sixty-four inexperienced actors stood on the 100-year-old stage and accepted the first standing ovation of their lives. The furious applause rang with pride, a little amazement and the appreciation of an audience that had been, most of all, entertained.

The 21-year-old director, Rod Lathim, was relieved. *Circus of Life* had been a one shot performance, the payoff for five months of work. By the time the show opened, it had not only drawn in the director and cast, but teachers and staff at local schools, Rod's parents, dozens of volunteers and 660 audience members. Though the performance was over, they had all embarked on the adventure that would be Access Theatre.

Circus of Life was a unique product of faith, talent, and not knowing any better. Rod answered a classified ad and was hired by the City of Santa Barbara Recreation Department to involve developmentally disabled students from local facilities in a talent show. He immediately threw out the idea ("I hate talent shows") and sold his employers on an original musical that he would write – a circus of life with a part for everybody.

It would be performed at the Lobero,

he decided, at that time *the* legitimate stage in town. The performance would be a benefit for Special Olympics and have a champagne intermission. "I was thinking big," he says. "I didn't see limitations."

Rod wrote a loose script, and with co-director Darcy Fluitt went into rehearsal at five locations across town. Each group of six to eighteen actors learned their songs and dances – as lion tamers, jugglers, and marionettes in love – and Rod put all the scenes together in the days before opening night.

"It was a series of little disasters in rehearsals," Rod remembers. "It was a matter of them learning and me learning what I could get, how far I could push them. The key was to break everything down into chewable bites. Everybody had their five seconds, or five minutes, whatever it was that they could handle and they knew it backwards, and when all the pieces went together like a jigsaw it worked. For one woman my goal with her was just to get her on and off stage. That was her triumph goal – just make it on and off stage and stay alive.

"People were looking at me thinking 'what in the world does he think he's gonna do?' They were anticipating chaos, or embar-

rassment." But the show started to come together. Costumes were borrowed from the well-stocked trunk of 80-year-old costumer Fran Grobben; a Los Angeles business donated part of the set; professional artist Susan Warren designed the poster.

Local television and stage actor Hank Underwood agreed to join the cast as the Ringmaster; his stature in the eyes of the actors convinced them that this was the big time. "There was an incredible camaraderie with this group," Rod says, "I think they all knew that they were doing something a lot of people thought they couldn't do, and they were proud of that."

"They got out of it an ability to *do*," Sister Trinitas remembers of her students. "So many times developmentally disabled children don't think they can *do* anything, and like with everything, most of us will work to the expectations of others. Those kids found out they had talents they could share with others. And when it was over their reaction was, 'we were *good*.' And yes they were."

"The Recreation Department staff kept saying we had no idea you could do this, we didn't expect this," Rod remembers. "And the other payoff was seeing the kids faces, they

Bobbie Hammerstrom, *Circus of Life*, 1979

were just bustin'. For some of them it was maybe the most exciting thing that will ever happen to them in their lives. We dashed people's expectations of their clients, children, and students."

And together they sowed the seeds of Access Theatre.

———

The next morning Rod was out of a job, the project complete, the meager funding spent. "Details," he concluded. He started writing the next show – an abstract musical that would explore serious issues in the lives of the actors he had come to know.

Grants from a local restaurant and the Santa Barbara Council for the Retarded made *Through Our Eyes* a reality; it opened on May 1, 1980 at the Lobero, almost exactly a year after *Circus of Life*. Like *Circus* it drew on the talents of volunteers, and through a chance meeting it brought Michael Douglas, the company's most ardent celebrity supporter, onto the scene.

Through Our Eyes featured sixty-three developmentally disabled actors ranging in age from eight to forty-eight. Through impressionistic dance, music and theatrical vignettes they talked about their lives and feelings, and how it felt to be labeled "handicapped." Rod's script and lyrics were built through interviews, based on the actors' answers – in many cases their exact words. The result was candid, avant garde and very theatrical.

"I wanted to explore the experience of living with a disability from their perspective, as opposed to society's definitions and labels," Rod says, "how *they* thought they were limited and discriminated against. What their dreams were. It was a taboo subject then to talk about the realities. It wasn't cool in 1980 to talk about disability when there were people with disabilities in the room."

"It was our chance to speak," remembers Laura Winter, a high school junior at the time she appeared in *Through Our Eyes*. "I wanted more people to understand that we're not to be, you know, closed up. I mean we're just as normal as anybody else is. We may have a few problems but that doesn't give people a right to close us off. So I felt that was a real important message and I think we got that point across.

"For me, I'm a slow learner, I walk with a limp, I've got scoliosis, I've got cerebral palsy, but all those put together I still don't feel

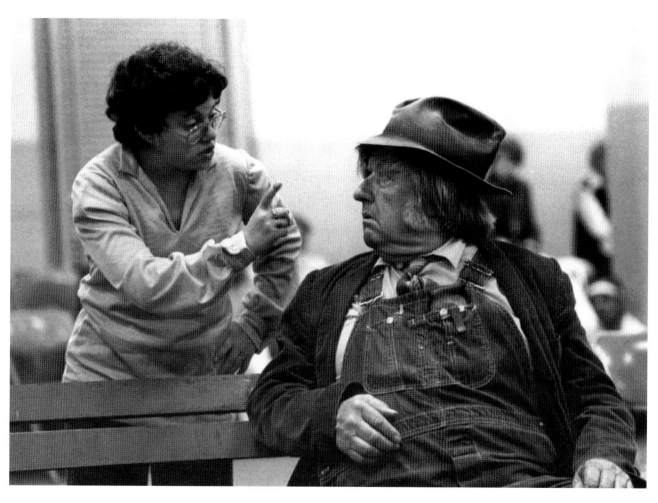

Cathy Lodge, Hank Underwood, *Through Our Eyes*, Lobero Theatre, 1980

"He could sing 'til the cows came home,"
Rod recalls of actor Dennis Subica *(right)*, a
developmentally disabled man who enlivened
four early productions including *Through Our
Eyes* with a voice that reminded critic John
Dell of Anthony Newley.

"My job was being in the play and doing a
good job, singing with the piano," Dennis, now
47, remembers. "When I was a little boy I
liked to sing, singing songs and having a good
time. Made me feel great, made me feel real
happy. I stopped singing because I didn't know
the songs too well, and then I sang again. It
was real neat, it worked out beautifully, made
me feel real good.

"I remember the day of the performance.
Everybody came. They all clapped, they stood
up and applauded for me. They wanted more
action. I remember that. They said 'Look at
that star Dennis Subica, he's a real great
actor.' I did real good. I learned how to be an
actor and go up on stage and perform. I did
everything. Doing a good job. And taking a
bow. Oh I did everything.

"I wasn't scared, I was fine. I just told
myself 'Nothin' to be scared about, I'm just
gonna do the song with the piano like Rod
said.' I don't get stagefright. I'm cool, calm,
and collected."

"I remember Terry Talley *(at left)* was under threat of being kept home from rehearsal for acting up — he was using foul language. Missing rehearsal was the darkest punishment we could hold over the kids because they wanted it so badly. Terry played the truck driver, and I remember I had to stand there with a straight face and tell him 'Truck drivers do not use bad language.' The staff was cracking up, but I had to be very stern. I often wonder if he found out the truth about truck drivers."

Sister Trinitas
Administrator, St. Vincent's School

that I'm abnormal, I'm just as bright or brighter than the next person in the block."

In the play, Laura carried a tinkling bag that represented her identity, but also her differences from "the public." As the cast members surround her like animals and demand that she relinquish her bag, her character panics, the bag is thrown to the floor and the contents shatter with a crash.

"Yes, my life has been like that since day one," she says of the scene. "People have a hard time with me being different, me not being normal in their eyes. I might not have been the same as everybody else, and I wasn't able to relate to people sometimes, but they always figured it was my problem, that *I* was the problem. This play gave me the courage to speak out, to know that no matter what people think, in your heart you can feel that you're OK.

"It was a lot of work," she says of rehearsals. "I'd heard rumors, but you don't actually know what goes into plays until you're in one. But I just kept thinking about being able to tell the world about us, about all of us, all of our feelings.

"On stage I was scared to death, you think 'oh my gosh, can we really pull this off?' Then the day it's finished, you think 'my gosh I wish

this would go on and on.' It was such a fantastic feeling, such a high. Our group was people who were labeled dysfunctional, or abnormal, or emotionally disturbed. But when we were up there, people were taking a second look, and maybe they were saying, 'wait, we're not stupid and dumb, we're just as normal as anyone.'"

—·—

Three months after *Through Our Eyes* closed, production began for *Take A Card, Any Card*, an award-winning drama by Washington writer Martin Kimeldorf. For the first time, Rod held open auditions that drew from the theater community at large, and so moved the company away from being a theater for people with developmental disabilities.

"The parents and kids from the first two shows said 'why can't we just keep doing this?'" Rod says. "I never had a good answer for them. I always said to the parents, 'you *should* keep doing this – and I'll support you to get it going.' I personally couldn't keep doing it. I was not cut out as an individual to spend a lifetime, or really any more time, working exclusively with people with developmental disabilities. Because it takes massive doses of patience and adapting, constantly

"At first I found it difficult to expose a very private part of my being," wrote *Through Our Eyes* collaborator Lupe Olvera, whose words and stories were incorporated into the play, though her severe muscular dystrophy kept her from performing. "I felt it was necessary so that the abled public could understand that our experiences are not any different — only the circumstances are. It was absolutely thrilling to see some of my personal experiences come to life on the stage. I felt a part of a wider spectrum of humanity... and felt proud to have touched other human beings." The play was dedicated to Lupe, who died in 1981 still in her twenties.

Rehearsal, *Through Our Eyes*, 1980

"We were rehearsing and in walks Michael Douglas. I about died. He was...oh my gosh...I just remember how neat it was. In person he's a gracious caring man. Nothing like he is on the screen." Performer Laura Winter breathlessly recalls the day Douglas followed up on a chance meeting with Rod and visited a rehearsal of *Through Our Eyes*. Douglas stayed for two hours, and became a cornerstone of support for the company in the years that followed.

adapting the work to people's abilities. For my own artistic path I had to move on, I wanted to continue growing, to tackle work that was challenging for me as a director and writer and for the actors and audiences."

The 22 cast members for *Take A Card* were as diverse as the community, including five people who used wheelchairs and first-time actress Alice Parkinson, who is blind. Rod himself stepped into the role of a central character at the last minute when one actor suddenly dropped out.

The drama, an Epic Theatre style parable, tells the story of Pip, a child who was born a "selnoy" – a fictitious disability that stands, in the playwright's words, "for all persons who experience stigma, segregation, social and physical barriers."

The actors with disabilities form a kind of Greek Chorus; they maintain a Brechtian commentary on the proceedings, as Pip and his parents are initiated into the discriminatory world of school, hospital, and institution. "The drama was really of it's time," Kimeldorf says. "When I wrote it in 1979, there were very few plays that addressed these issues. At that time people were starting to talk more about non-whites and women, but there was

very little discussion about civil rights for people with disabilities."

Kimeldorf's script freely wove satire, farce, melodrama and tragedy to express tough realities about how society treats people with disabilities. Rod expanded on this poetic style, presenting Kimeldorf's words in rhythmic beats and extrapolating some of the dialogue into lyrics. He commissioned impressionistic music by 20-year-old composer Mark Henderson, who would go on to compose many of Access Theatre's best-known works.

"We were very proud of that show," recalls Theresa Peretik, who uses a wheelchair since becoming quadriplegic in a hang-gliding accident, and who appeared in leading roles for the company through 1983. "It was beautiful. Very avant garde. The rhythms made it very artistic, and I think easier to watch. People might have thought it was overstated, but actually it was very realistic. These things really happen. They have happened to me."

Take A Card, Any Card brought the company under the non-profit umbrella of Santa Barbara's Independent Living Resource Center, a non-profit service organization for people with disabilities. It marked the beginning of a relationship between the two organizations

Pip (Paul Davies), *Take A Card, Any Card*, Lobero Theatre, 1980

Chorus, *Take A Card, Any Card*, Lobero Theatre, 1980. "It tackles a major social issue that has been totally disregarded in the theater, faces it head-on and smashes it. And let the sacred cows fall where they may."

John Dell
Theater Critic
Santa Barbara News-Press

that would last until 1988, and introduced Rod to a big part of his job: fundraising. His time was soon split between creating art and seeking funding. "I approached it with a certain innocence and enthusiasm," Rod says, "like 'nothin's gonna stop me now.' I found out it was much harder than it looked."

Take A Card was a time of firsts for the company – the first sign language interpretation, the first cast members who used wheelchairs, the first Velcro for costumes ("a lifesaver," Rod recalls). It was also the first time for audience "talkback" sessions, which became an Access Theatre trademark – a natural outgrowth of the mission to create access for the audience.

"With talkbacks, you hope to get positive feedback because you want to hear good things," Rod says of the sessions, "But you also want to hear what doesn't work, because there are things that you would never guess are not working for people. I don't think theater has to stop at the curtain at the end of the show. It's people to people communication, and I think it just makes the experience richer if the audience has a chance to have a voice other than just clapping."

What audiences say with that voice has

ranged from "why don't you tie that guys hands down?" about an actor with cerebral palsy, to, more commonly, spontaneous testimonials. "They say things like 'I'll never see a person with a disability the same way again; I'll never see *myself* the same way again," Rod explains. "It's spine tingling to see how an hour and half in the theater can change someone's outlook."

—·—

In 1981, the International Year of the Disabled, Rod mobilized for his first big musical. Confident in the abilities of young composer Mark Henderson, Rod wanted to return to a theatrical form he knew and loved – musical theater. With his roommate from college, Michael Hughs, he began to write an original revue, based on the premise, "given an empty theater with its sets, costumes, lights, and technical magic, what would you do?" The answer was *Footlight Fantasy*.

"The auditions were like a Fellini movie," says independent living specialist Marty Kinrose, who brought a vanload of his clients to try out for the new musical. "You had huge numbers of people of all ages. And talk about the broad spectrum of abilities, you

Rehearsal, *Footlight Fantasy*, 1981

Gina Dyson,
Footlight Fantasy,
1981

had people who had no speech, you had singers who used wheelchairs, you had people who were underemployed local actors and actresses just looking for roles, you really had such a wide gamut of people and needs, attitudes and egos. And Rod – this 22-year-old kid – was somehow negotiating with them and handling them all."

To his surprise, Marty, a former theme park character and Dixieland tuba player, was cast alongside his clients and began his long association with the company.

"Rod was able to pick from a person's most minute ability." Marty recalls. "If the person was good at brushing their teeth he could turn that into something that they could do on the stage. If there was somebody he just couldn't find something for he would involve them as a crew person. These productions did that for people. It gave them a sense of belonging and it really pumped up their self esteem."

"There was a basic foundation of acceptance and love. You walked in the door and you were greeted and people were happy to see you. The environment was more tuned in to people's needs, so there wasn't going to be all the typical discomforts and barriers that exist in the community at large. But expectations were also high. You had a job to do, so you were challenged."

Footlight Fantasy was the first Access Theatre show to tour; response from audiences and critics was enthusiastic. "A must for anyone who cares anything at all about the theater," one critic gushed. "This is what they made theater for," wrote another, "not just to keep you off the streets or to mildly amuse you...but to grab you, to touch you, to actually make you different. And better."

—·—

Like so many things in Access Theatre's history, the next production was built on pure serendipity.

In the summer of 1981, Michael Douglas arranged for Rod and colleague Michael Hughs to travel to the Eugene O'Neill Theater Center in Connecticut, where the National Theatre of the Deaf was in residence. They returned home eager to experiment with sign language.

Access Theatre's first deaf actress, Lori Hennessey, had joined the company earlier in the year. Rod filled out the cast of his new show with five hearing actors, two interpreters, and two more deaf actors, including a precocious six-year-old, Solomon Smaniotto,

They soared together

In joyous flight

Their feathers glowed

A brilliant white

There were two sea birds

Like you and me

Left comfort shores

For open sea

"I had never really worked so closely with someone on anything,"
recalled deaf dancer Lori Hennessey of her duet with deaf partner
Michael Spencer. "We had to find similar rhythms and a wavelength
to get the chemistry between us. I never really thought about the
counts, I practiced internalizing the rhythm, and thought about the
meaning of the music and the song."

Footlight Fantasy, 1981

Solomon Smaniotto *(at right)* was Access Theatre's youngest
performer; he joined the company of *Signing Off* when he was six
years old, toured the western states with *Finger Talk* when he was
just eight and performed with the company until he was eleven. His
mother remembers him as a bright, frustrated, isolated child, given to
tantrums, who blossomed in the stimulating environment of
the theater.

Solomon went on to the Riverside School of the Deaf in Southern
California, auditioned for the nighttime soap *Dallas* and was cast
as a regular for one season. Seen below with his *Dallas* co-star on
Entertainment Tonight, he soon tired of the Hollywood scene, entered
college at the University of California at San Diego, and continued to
pursue performance art and writing. "Being in Access Theatre was
like growing up with two families," Solomon remembers. "It helped
me to feel whole and positive, and to find what we all have in
common, which is our heart."

who became a cast and audience favorite. With input from the cast, Rod and co-director Susan Warren created *Signing Off*, a musical revue performed in sign and voice-interpreted for the sign language impaired.

"We got to *play* and do things we'd never done before with the language," Rod says, "we put sign language on a pedestal with that show. The focus was on the language, this visual, full-bodied communication."

For the first time the actors were paid – $5 to $10 a performance. *Signing Off* toured to 20 venues, including Disneyland for the Very Special Arts Festival; it was presented as a benefit hosted by Michael Douglas at Santa Barbara's Victoria Street Theater in November of 1981. The company's modest funding base was also expanding to include foundations and state and local agencies.

In this year Rod, who had always networked locally, began speaking at a handful of national conferences and workshops. The company was just two years old, but was already a pioneer, blending the talents of disabled and non-disabled, deaf, hearing, blind, and sighted actors.

The foundation was set, but no one could imagine what would follow, and how many people and lives would connect and overlap on Access Theatre's eighteen-year journey.

"Crispy-clean, magical, professional theater.
Signing Off is ensemble theater at its best."

Helena Minulta
National Theatre of the Deaf

Peter McCorkle, Suzy Beckman and cast, "Gorilla," *Signing Off*, 1981

"...theater of life, dignity, and acceptance." *Los Angeles Times*, 1983

stagestruck

Stage Struck remains in the hearts and memories of participants and audiences, as perhaps no other Access Theatre show. A big, joyful musical, it was at once the climax of what the company had been building and the end of an era – the last all-volunteer show, the last big cast, and the last time some of the actors would perform with the company. It was also the show that first brought Access Theatre to international attention, and it cracked open a door of opportunity that the company would burst through in the following decade.

It was the biggest thing Access Theatre had ever done. It featured a Mickey Rooney/Judy Garland plotline magnified by ten, with more than 30 cast and crew members, 18 musicians, and a small army of behind-the-scenes volunteers and sponsors. It ran on pure heart and youthful stamina. It led to four weddings among participants. It was, as one cast member said, "the ultimate grassroots musical," written, composed, staged and choreographed on a budget of pinched pennies and donated sweat. The critics said "exhilarating," "enchanting," or simply "wow."

Stage Struck was first mounted in the fall of 1982, then expanded and restaged the following spring. It would travel to Palm Springs, earn the attention of the Princess Grace Foundation USA and bring together the company's first board of directors. Everyone involved dreamed big, and the bittersweet truth was they got their wish. The company was no longer community theater; it had turned a corner. Awards, international tours, and television would all come over the next decade, while budgets would eventually increase twenty-fold. And though for some actors it was their last production with the company, many more people found Access Theatre through that show – all of them dizzy with the potential, and stagestruck to the core.

That's how it appears, looking back. At the time, it just seemed like it might be fun, a big, crazy idea built on a brainstorm of "what if..." What if the under-appreciated stage crew saved a show? What if the costumes were hot pink? What if we wrote songs? What if we said "hey gang let's do a show," and *everyone* was welcome?

———

On the day of auditions, Marty Kinrose, an independent living consultant and Access Theatre veteran, picked up Stephen Day at his new apartment. The van was nearly full with six of Marty's other clients, and they all sang with the radio on the way to the First Congregational Church.

Inside, some 60 people of all ages and abilities trouped up one by one to stand next to music director Shelley Rink at the piano. They sang Lerner and Lowe, they sang Oscar Hammerstein, they sang the "Star Spangled Banner" or "Happy Birthday" if they had nothing prepared.

Stephen watched the others and grew confident that his voice would get him a part in the chorus. He'd sung some glee club. He didn't expect a second lead, or a solo. But he was ready for the challenge if it came. Very carefully, he rolled up to the piano, praying he wouldn't make some jerky movement and spoil his chances.

With his father in the service and his mother living with polio, Stephen's cerebral palsy had kept him in institutions since he was twelve. His CP was categorized as "severe," and affected his breathing and motor control. He could not use his legs and he jumped involuntarily at any sudden sound – a "startle mechanism," part of his life with CP. Yet, he'd lived on his own for almost a year now. He'd definitely take a bigger part if it was offered.

In thirteen years in institutions Stephen had been "completely taken care of," he says "down to what I wore, what I ate." By the time he was a teenager he was ready to rebel – sneaking out of the facility at night, or ordering pizza delivery when corned beef hash was on the menu.

His venial uprisings were tolerated, until he decided to move out on his own. While Stephen traveled back and forth to town for eight months of classes in "independent living," the medical director of his facility applied to have him declared legally incompetent. "The staff thought I was wasting my

Why do we do what we do?

Why are we members of the cast and crew?

Oh it's not for the almighty buck

Guess we're just staaage struck!

Cast and crew, *Stage Struck*, Lobero Theatre, 1983

time," he remembers, "But I knew enough to know that they couldn't really stop me even though they wouldn't help me.

"I'd only seen one, maybe two other people try to leave before. It's very difficult, not just physically. You're told things like 'you're not going to make it on your own, you're going to be hurt or disappointed, or even worse you could die.' Unless you're prepared for hearing that and just sort of ignoring it you'll be talked out of it. And that happened a lot. People got talked out of it. Because the nursing staff at that time was of the old school of protecting. People that were disabled needed to be *protected*. Because the world out there was too tough for them to manage. But I was just existing, it was not a life. And I thought if I don't take chances with my life, then it's not mine."

A year after moving out on his own, Stephen was managing his household and starting a second college degree. He was excited and a little scared about being cast in a solo part in *Stage Struck*. "The show was another step out in my independent life," he says. "It was part of being 'out there' to be on stage. And I felt I was doing things that everyone else was doing. I wasn't doing a 'special thing' anymore, a special group, special classes. I was doing it pretty much the way everybody else was. I was as much of an actor as I could be – singing, dancing, being free.

"I was integrated with non-disabled actors as well. And I *felt* integrated because I didn't just do singing, I was allowed to move, which I was terrified to do at first. I don't think Rod ever said, 'I don't think you should do that – too tough on you. I'll give it to someone else.' I'm sure there were times he wondered, but he never showed it. He had high standards for me and it was hard, but I thought 'he wants me to shine and be just as good or better than everybody else.'

"After rehearsals I would be so wound up I couldn't sleep. I knew it was going to be powerful, I knew it couldn't help but affect people. Knowing that excited me, and so I just told myself like I always do – 'go for it. Don't chicken out.'"

—·—

Stage Struck was a case of art imitating life, a thinly disguised version of the real Access Theatre. The story line was cheerfully implausible: the stuck-up able-bodied cast of "Flamingos on Ice," goes on strike; the dedicated disabled backstage crew saves the day. The able-bodied diva is replaced with an understudy who moves in a wheelchair; the hearing boy marries the deaf girl. It was classic musical comedy fantasy. But the energy and "can do" spirit that audiences saw on stage was very realistic, and completely disarming. The story had nothing to do with disability, except to fly in the face of it. Behind the scenes, disability issues were just part of getting the job done.

"We just added it into the mix," Rod said. "That might mean common courtesy, like raising your hand to speak, so you can be interpreted, or maybe helping someone go to the bathroom. From the beginning we got the needs on the table. Maybe it was 'don't come up behind me and start talking because it makes me jump,' or 'I have a urine bag and it's concealed here, so please don't hit my leg because you'll make a mess.' Or, 'I can only roll myself around in my chair for this long until I poop out,' or 'please don't talk too fast it takes me a little bit longer to get it.' We just tried to get all the needs, concerns and fears, and throw them out there. Then it's OK, it's done. It's not a mystery.

"The theater should be an environment where you can bare all, take risks, communicate, speak for yourself, create, grow, experiment. You can't do that when there are secrets, especially if you roll around in the secret. We're an ensemble, and you have to know your weaknesses and your strengths. That's how you work as a team."

———

Every day cast members gathered from school or day jobs at gas stations, restaurants or accounting firms. Some waited for Marty or Theresa to pick them up in accessible vans, some took the bus or walked. From all over town they converged on rehearsal with the same goal, but entirely personal reasons for being there.

Kathyrn Voice was a 21-year-old opera performance student at the Music Academy of the West, and auditioned for *Stage Struck* the second time it was produced. Music director Shelley Rink remembers a tall, quiet young woman with a voice that knocked them out. "We were standing there with our mouths open. She had appeared out of nowhere with this voice."

Katie's appearance at the audition was no accident. She had been in the audience the first time *Stage Struck* was presented, a reluctant spectator who was avoiding unresolved feelings about her childhood with her deaf sister Suzy.

"My life had taken me away from home and deep into music – almost as far away from my sister as I could get," Katie says. "That night was an epiphany. I had never quite seen a show like this. I was just astounded. So I found myself wanting to do more than a standing ovation. I had this really strong urge to stand on the arm rests of the chair to get even higher in my praise. It was a real moment of freedom for me. And I thought 'why did I wait so long to see their shows? Now I understand.' It turned me away from feelings of guilt and atonement about my relationship with my sister to feelings of celebration. When I saw deaf, hearing and disability cultures supporting each other on stage, I realized it is never too late to build two-way communication. We build on where we stand."

Sign language soon became a central focus of Katie's life. She threw herself into the company and into sign language classes with castmate Peter Robertson. It was a very different environment from the self-protective world of classical music.

"With opera, I had often let my own nerves get in the way of my performance. I always thought 'my pre-performance conditions need to be perfect, and if everything is just so, I'll do well.' I think with *Stage Struck* I learned to let go of that limiting attitude. *Stage Struck* was such a metaphor of ensemble strength and mutual support. In the end, the sum was greater than its individual parts, so I let go of my self-centered fears.

"It's just a small thing really, but I think it's a common awakening for a lot of performers who work with Access Theatre. I stopped thinking about myself and my performance all the time and I started thinking more about other people. I found that performance took on a whole new register to me, much richer, more of a living exchange between the audience and the performers. I felt I could drop my guard and be more real. And with that, some of the funniest, most amazing magic does happen."

—·—

Stage Struck was a magnet, and all over town people started to help. One of the fathers, Joe Hennessey, engineered the big revolving set in his spare time. Rod's parents

"What I love about theater," says company member Remi Sandri, "is that theater says — hopefully — it's all possible. That this is who you are today, these are the choices you made to get to this point, but inside of you is also this person and that person and that person. So theater can be a celebration of what it means to be a human being and all its facets, which are infinitely cut. We usually live our lives on only a few facets, and that's our comfort zone, but to step outside of that, it can teach you compassion. Access Theatre puts you outside those comfort zones and there's a real opening up, a feeling of 'and *this* too, this is part of what it means to be a human being.'"

Company warm-up, *Stage Struck*, 1983

sewed, drove, and fed people. "I remember lots of potato salad," Kathy Lathim says with a laugh. Local businesses donated typesetting, advertising and lumber; the program acknowledged nearly 200 donations of money and in-kind support. Rod's collaborators continued to surprise him with artwork, costumes, innovations and ideas.

"We lived it, ate it, slept it. It was a pure act of creation from start to finish," remembers co-writer and art director Susan Warren. The show even drew in complete strangers, one in particular who would get Access Theatre its first big tour and an introduction to the unlikely audience of Palm Springs society.

Dave Hopson remembers himself as a lonely bachelor/salesman/former actor out for an evening jog after a discouraging day. He ended up outside the Lobero Theatre, intrigued by a cluster of girls in pink feather boas. He slipped inside and sat unnoticed at the back of the theater, fascinated by the assortment of performers in wheelchairs, and people talking with their hands. "There was an excitement, an electricity," he remembers. "The orchestra revved up and the dress rehearsal began. It just took me away." Two hours later he was glued to his seat as the curtain came

down. "It was unlike anything I had seen in New York, or in my own professional career. I had lost myself in the acting. It wasn't 'disabled' theater. It was totally accessible theater." Dave found Rod in the post-performance chaos and made a proposition.

Two months later, Katie Voice was packing pretty much everything from her closet into an orange VW bug for the weekend tour to Palm Springs. Stephen was once again squeezed into Marty Kinrose's van. They joined the company convoy for the 200-mile pilgrimage. "We descended like a three ring circus," Marty remembers.

Dave Hopson was ready. In the months leading up to the performance, he and his family had formed a coalition with associates in the medical community. They arranged the funding, the theater, the publicity, even the big BBQ that was waiting for the cast in the parking lot of the motel where they were staying. Kirk and Michael Douglas hosted a benefit dinner, audiences cheered. *Stage Struck* was a hit on the road.

Rod and company were exhausted. "I don't think Rod would be alive today if he kept doing it the way he did *Stage Struck*," Marty says. "Not only was he putting together

Stephen Day *(center left)*, and
Mark Janisch *(center right)*
with Kirk Douglas and cast,
Palm Springs, 1983

"I knew I would like being on the stage.

I like being in the spotlight.

It's kind of hard to get thrills in this position,

so you take what you can get."

Theresa Peretik Bulne was a confirmed thrillseeker, single mother, and one of the few women apprentices in the Brotherhood of Carpentry, when her hanglider veered headfirst into a cliff on Bastille Day, 1977. "I remember the first time I saw a hanglider. I got chills, tears, I wanted to do it so badly. People would ask me, 'aren't you afraid?' and I said no. I figured I'd either break all my bones and they'd mend or I'd die. I didn't know about quadriplegia. I don't think it would have stopped me."

Theresa joined Access Theatre in 1980 for *Take A Card, Any Card*, and played the second female lead in *Stage Struck*, as the understudy who gets her big chance to be a star.

"With theater I found another high. At the curtain call when we received a standing ovation from 600 people, my blood again ran quickly through my veins," she wrote shortly after *Stage Struck* opened. "It's really give and take," she says, "you give your performance and they give back applause. It's a pretty good exchange."

Theresa went on to perform in other local plays and in an episode of *Cagney and Lacey*, but found that professional opportunities were scarce; she eventually married and stopped performing.

Marty Kinrose *(with interpreter Peter Robertson)* wrote his own song, "Marty's Blues" for his role as the beleaguered director of *Stage Struck*'s show within a show, "Flamingos on Ice." "There was always room for everybody's creativity," he says.

Stage Struck, Lobero Theatre, 1982

a huge production, he was also the publicity guy, the designer, he was the everything, *and* he was the guy who had to raise money so he could pay his own salary and for everything else. He had great support, awesome support, from his family, friends, and volunteers, but he was still the guy. No one in their right mind would have done it. But we were all a lot younger then. And we were possessed."

The volunteer spirit that infused *Stage Struck* succeeded beyond everyone's expectations and gave the young company a push towards professionalism, toward an ever-expanding audience, and away from some of the people it had first been created to serve. From now on casts and crew would be paid, but they would be smaller, and there was less room for beginners.

"It wasn't a conscious thing," Rod remembers. "But we could not afford to do it on that scale again. I didn't want to leave anyone behind, but I knew I was going to and I did, and it hurt."

After *Stage Struck* closed, some of the most memorable Access Theatre personalities would continue only as audience members, including Stephen Day, who went on to become a disability advocate and popular speaker, and never stopped looking for another chance to be on the stage.

———

Backstage before every performance, the cast and crew stood in a circle holding hands. Rod started a note that would build into a harmony and pound through the backstage. Minutes later Shelley Rink lifted her baton in the orchestra pit and the overture started.

"Sometimes the sound of it almost made me cry," Stephen says, "it was that feeling of 'this is it, here we go.' And I was changing; no one could see it but I was getting ready to go on stage." Stephen's solo "Stage Fright," came in the second act. "It was my moment to shine," he says, "and I just told myself, 'whatever else is going on, it will keep, just focus on this.' I had to put all my concentration into keeping my body calm."

Opening night, under the hot lights and facing his first big audience, Stephen began to hyperventilate. "I was terrified that Rod would try to stop the show, but he didn't. I was afraid my *mom* would try to stop it, but my sister kept telling her – 'he's only acting.' And I'm thinking 'I am gonna get through this, I will not pass out.' Because you could not let the cast down.

"I looked *forward* to going to rehearsal," recalls Peter McCorkle *(above)*. "Whatever happened in the day, however I was feeling, I could not *wait* to go and do this." At 19, McCorkle starred in the first production of *Stage Struck*, and choreographed the second, expanding on Mike Downey's original choreography and adding three new numbers including the show-stopping "Fairyland of Love," which he led with partner Kathy Spang *(above)*. "For the Palm Springs performance, Kathy had a riding injury and had to have a gurney in the wings so she could lay down when she wasn't on stage," Peter recalls of his partner. "She was the ultimate trooper. When it was time to go on we'd just throw her into her wheelchair and away we went."

Nearly every Access Theatre show was composed from scratch — a total of
nine original musicals, two musical reviews, and four original plays, all with
musical elements.

Rod composed the songs and wrote the lyrics for his first two musicals, and
then in 1981 met a young musician and aspiring composer, Mark Colin Henderson
[right]. Mark could not read or write music, but when he sat at the old piano in
Rod's living room and played his melodies, Rod was convinced.

For *Stage Struck*, Mark wrote eleven songs, from be-bop production numbers to
love ballads, and Los Angeles lyricist Connie Samovitz wrote the words. The
show took shape in Connie's living room, Rod's garage, and leaning over Mark's
rickety piano.

But once the compositions were ready, no one knew how to write them down,
orchestrate the arrangements, and fill in the transitions. Rod hired UCSB
composition graduate Shelley Rink *[right]*, and found the perfect support for his
composer. Shelley called in local arrangers, patiently rehearsed the
inexperienced singers into a cohesive chorus, and conducted the live orchestra
in performance.

The results were so good that the company decided to record the soundtrack;
Santa Barbara Sound agreed to donate studio off-hours for the project. Squeezed
into 3 a.m. gaps in the studio schedule, the Access performers finished the first
cast album — and set a precedent that would be continued with every show.
Today, Mark has a formal music degree, and partner Gregory Kuhn scores
commercials and films. They have an orchestra at their fingertips, thanks to
MIDI computer technology — a tool that was essentially unheard of when *Stage
Struck* was composed.

Stephen Day and cast, "Stage Fright,"

Stage Struck, Lobero Theatre, 1983

"It was completely energy draining but it felt good, and I remember when we stood at the curtain call, I knew a portion of that applause was for me. That was an incredible high.

"This," Stephen told the *L.A. Times* shortly after opening night, "is one of the three greatest things in my life. Number One was being able to leave an institution and live on my own. This may be the second greatest. But in case I ever get married or something I'm leaving room. So, this is *at least* the third greatest.

"The memories are rich and so strong," he says now. "If you could have seen me. I made my mark in the world. How many people can say that? If I became a recluse tomorrow – which isn't very likely – nothing could take that away. I felt like somebody special just for being in that company."

Four weddings.
Access board member Dave Hopson and his brother Randy met their wives when they all worked together on *Stage Struck*'s Palm Springs tour. Marty Kinrose married castmate Karen Rink. Co-writer Susan Warren met and married a member of the audience, deaf advocate Larry Littleton. Above, Lori Hennessey and Remi Sandri perform the show's wedding ballad "Starting from Today." Lobero Theatre, 1983

Cast, *Stage Struck*, 1983

Cast, "I'm Always Chasing Rainbows," *Finger Talk*

Lori speaking from the heart

Pullman, Washington was a beige and gray town wrapped in a gray winter, when nine troubadours burst into the local diner in crayola-bright costumes and high top sneakers. Hands and eyes flashed as they signed to each other and laughed about the snow, and people looked up from their coffee.

Later at the Sunnyside elementary school auditorium, a single deaf student – the only one in the school – sat in raptured disbelief as the visitors performed in a language he completely understood, his native tongue, American Sign Language.

When the other kids laughed, Chris did too – at the unicorn who ate the flowers, the Blob, and Jimmy Jet who watched TV 'til his eyes were frozen wide. He was pulled up on stage during the tiger skit, and after the show, when his schoolmates crowded around him with questions, he was no longer ignored, but a sudden celebrity with a very cool language.

From the stage in Pullman, and in Moscow, Idaho, and in towns across Oregon and California, actress Lori Hennessey looked out at the intent faces and the small cluster of deaf students in every *Finger Talk* audience. "I saw myself," she says, and the teenage performer modified her dream of joining the National Theater of the Deaf.

"I decided to become a teacher," she remembers, and 10 years later, with a degree from the California State University at Northridge, she began to teach deaf children what she had first learned on the Access Theatre stage.

———

Lori Hennessey joined Access Theatre in 1981, a shy and socially frustrated 7th-grader mainstreamed into a local junior high school. She had gradually given up trying to be part of the "popular" crowd at school. She didn't make drill team or the class play, and soon withdrew from what she was sure would be more disappointment.

Even so, when the school announced that a director had come scouting for performers, she was cautiously excited. Her school interpreter Francine Buker went with her to meet Rod Lathim. For both Lori and Fran, it was a life-changing introduction; over the next decade, Access Theatre became a central part of their lives.

It was also important for Rod, who had no sign language experience at the time. "I remember sitting out on the lawn with her at the first rehearsal and thinking 'I have *got* to learn how to sign, and *fast*.' It was comical, I was gesturing and miming and mouthing like a stupid hearing person." Rod began lessons immediately, eager to learn Lori's language. "I didn't want to be separate from her," he says, "none of us did. She was so shy and so reserved, closed even. But we just dangled theater in front of her and she bit."

"I knew I wanted to be something big," Lori says, "but I was very isolated. My parents were wonderful, but that's not enough. I had really sort of resigned myself to being limited in my opportunities because of my deafness. I

thought 'OK then, just drop it – that's what I have then, so just settle for less.' But Access Theatre taught me a different way. They said 'no, don't settle for less!'

"There were very few people in my life who put high expectations on me and expected that I could do well. Most people would make things easier for me because of my deafness, they would take care of me, speak for me, I didn't have very much input on my own part. I was well taken care of, but with Rod I learned to take care of myself so I have to say thanks to him.

"Before Rod came into my life I didn't really accept my deafness. I'd wish that I was hearing and sometimes I would act like I was hearing, or I would tell my peers that 'oh yeah, oh I like music, yeah.' I'd study all the names of the musicians so I would know what they were talking about. But really when I think about it, it was never a part of me. I was denying my own identity. I just didn't know myself yet. And I knew almost nothing about how to have relationships with other people. But through the theater, I was going to find out."

—·—

Finger Talk was a bilingual revue –

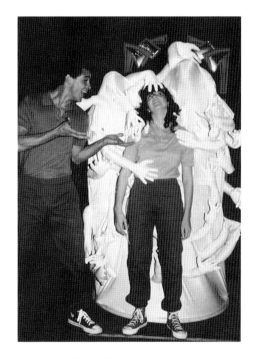

Victor Torres, Lori Hennessey, The Blob,

"Do the Blob," *Finger Talk*

On tour.

Peter McCaffrey,
Francine Buker, Rod
Lathim, Peter Robertson,
Bo Ayer, Kathryn Voice,
Victor Torres, Lori
Hennessey, Peter
McCorkle and Solomon
Smaniotto.
Finger Talk, 1984

Chris and cast, "Ladies First," *Finger Talk*,
Sunnyside Elementary School, Pullman, Washington, 1984

Victor Torres, Kathryn Voice, Peter McCorkle, *Finger Talk*

written in sign language and "voice inter-preted" for hearing audiences. At 45 minutes long it was just right for touring, packed with songs, humor, whimsical soft sculpture, and the energy of signing Mouseketeers on a mission.

"We were like kids pulling things out of our toy box, it had that kind of pace," remembers cast member Katie Voice. But in addition to the comedy, the show had three poignant monologues that touched on deaf culture and drew cheers of empathy from hearing and deaf audiences alike. Katie spoke of overcoming her isolation from her deaf sister; Victor Torres made a charismatic case for learning another language – *his* language.

For her monologue, Lori expressed the frustration and embarrassment of oral speech classes from her childhood. She recalled her teacher's inexplicable enthusiasm when she managed to pronounce the letter 'k' – a meaningless achievement made humiliating when she was paraded next door to demonstrate in front of a hearing class. "I had no idea why this was supposed to be so important," she recalls. "It was all very much by rote, doing it again and again, without ever really internalizing what language *was*, what it was for.

"In my monologue, I wanted to say that

speech alone was not a language. I was very frustrated at how many people out there held a pathological view of deafness, thinking that people who had good speech skills would have a better life. I wanted them to understand that deaf children *have* a language, and that sign language *is* a language.

"Some people had a very hard time understanding that and I think we did a lot to educate people. And we were reaching deaf children too, which was very, very important to me. In some cases, I was the first deaf adult they had ever met and they were surprised. They'd look at me and say 'are you deaf too?' It was almost as if in their minds, they thought that when they grew up they would become hearing. And I realized how alone they were and how much they needed interaction with other people who spoke their language and who could be role models."

For herself, Lori was gradually learning what speech classes had never taught her, and what her isolation from other sign speakers had excluded her from. "In my life I had never been able to observe language in use. I wasn't listening to language 24 hours a day the way hearing students do. At home, my parents signed, but they tended to only when speaking

Fingertalkin' feelin' cool

Fingerwalkin' on finger fuel

Fingertalkin' now watch my eyes

They're gonna tell you what words can disguise

Company, *Finger Talk*, Lobero Theatre, 1983

directly to me. So I wasn't learning about communicating. In the theater, I could study language as it happened in front of me. I could observe how people related to each other, how they communicated, and I learned a *lot*."

Fran and the other interpreters would translate everything, even passing conversations, so Lori and the other deaf cast members could "eavesdrop" the way hearing people can. "It sounds like such a small thing," Lori says. "But it was everything. I began to understand the dynamics of relationships.

"They would *find* ways to communicate with me, and I would *find* ways to communicate with them. It was a very alive experience. Inspirational."

———

In a restaurant in Solvang, California, the waitress faced a table of ten. No one spoke a word with their voices, even those who could, but signed across the table and wrote their orders on napkins.

The *Finger Talk* cast included three deaf performers and three sign language interpreters, who helped everyone else on the tour learn to sign. Almost like a secret club with it's own language, the company grew close, performing the show off-and-on over a three-year period. They traveled all over the western states, a carpool caravan full of bold and funny gypsies, who were becoming best friends.

"We found out about 'accessible,'" remembers Fran. "Especially going on tour. How does a deaf person get room service? A wakeup call? Slip a piece of paper under the door, 'wake up?' Smoke alarms? We got to the first hotel and lo and behold, no caption box on the TV. Bummer. So none of us watched TV. It wasn't perfect – sometimes the hearing cast members had to be educated. I remember one time there was a mini-revolution and the deaf cast members came to us to say 'don't leave anyone out.' It was intense, but I think it just brought us closer."

Most of the cast can still remember the *Finger Talk* wave, a stiff-fingered royalty-on-parade gesture, that resembles the sign for the color blue. They saw snow for the first time. They performed under nearly every type of circumstance – stepping on food in school cafeterias, or clearing rocks and laying blankets to perform in a dirt field. In unheated gymnasiums they ran laps and did calisthenics to Michael Jackson's "Thriller" to get warm enough to go on.

Company and kids
perform the *Finger Talk*
"wave." On tour, 1984

Victor Torres and cast, "Jimmy Jet," *Finger Talk*

61

"It was liberating for me as a performer," Katie remembers. "I just had to let go of my worries about the performance and just trust in the group. There was a kind of white-hot focus when we were together, and this power we could all draw upon. We really felt it in the warm up. Rod could really invoke a vision for us of why we were there. And though we were all so different he had a way of getting us to focus as a group.

"It was kind of the golden years," Katie remembers of the *Finger Talk* run. "It was the process even more than the product," adds Fran. "The touring was the most fun I ever had with a group of people. We were there for each other rain or shine, sick or healthy, we couldn't do it without every one of us."

The friendships lasted – Katie and Rod were at Fran's bedside when her triplet sons were delivered; Rod organized the cleanup when Fran's house burned, and everyone rallied when Lori's father died suddenly.

"We were all brothers and sisters," remembers Solomon Smaniotto, who was the youngest member of the cast at ten years old. "Through good and bad we were a family and we helped move the world towards peace, love, and understanding."

"It was the first time I had really laughed with people," Lori says, "really laughed at the same time they did, without always having to wait for the joke to be interpreted. It was very powerful for me. I really learned what a friendship was all about – how to develop listening skills, how to share, and how to be there for each other.

"The people I worked with in the theater opened my heart. I learned the power of universal language, not just English or sign language, but the language people use for the purpose of getting in touch with each other, that powerful tool that gives you the ability to express yourself and to be able to listen.

"That's what was given to me through the theater, and that's what I'm passing on to my students. I think it's the most important thing you can teach a child – not how to speak, not even a language, but how and *why* we communicate. That's what opens up the world. It did for me."

Lori Hennessey and cast, "Ladies First," *Finger Talk*

On sign language

Interpretation

bilingual

adj.: expressed in, knowing, or using two languages.

For Access Theatre, sign language was not only a stage convention, it was the living language of rehearsals, backstage, and tour. Cast and crew included both deaf and hearing individuals – a range of fluency from beginners to skilled interpreters to people who use sign as their first and primary language. The interplay among these individuals shaped the use of sign language throughout Access Theatre's history.

As with most things, the company found its own path with sign language. The old theater convention of placing an interpreter off to the side of the stage, at a podium or on a platform, was not the Access style. It left deaf audience members with a dilemma – watch the interpreter or watch the play. Instead, sign was woven into the fabric of Access Theatre's productions, and further into every aspect of how the company put on a show. Everyone who came through the door used or learned sign to

whatever their ability – they worked with it, played with it, and spoke it among themselves.

This was the obvious approach because sign language, in this case American Sign Language, *is* a language – a living, breathing, grammatically-defined language, native to some half a million North Americans. As distinct from English-coded sign languages (mostly developed by hearing educators), ASL is not based on English. Though a great many deaf people know and use English fluently, some ASL speakers have never learned English, and can neither read text nor understand the spoken language.

True ASL has nothing to do with English, or even words, but expresses concepts and images directly; an ASL sign denotes a thing, a feeling, an action or an idea, not a word. Yet linguistically ASL is just as complete as any spoken, word-based language, with detailed rules of syntax and grammar.

There are English-based sign dialects which represent English words through signs, and these have been incorporated into Access Theatre's translations. But it is ASL, the indigenous language of the deaf community, that most influenced Access Theatre's style. ASL is a visual and powerful theatrical tool, but more than that it carries the power of culture – deaf culture. Like any language, ASL has regional dialects, expressions, and slang. Like all language, it reflects a point of view, and adds another distinct voice to any production. And so the mingling of deaf and hearing language and culture affected Access Theatre's art and relationships, everything the company did.

Access Theatre was not, and did not try to be, deaf theater. Instead it was available to both deaf and hearing performers and audience members, and incorporated the voice of American Sign Language into the company's art and life.

———

Access Theatre first used sign language in late 1980, when interpreters from the Community Center on Deafness "shadow interpreted" the drama *Take A Card, Any Card*. As the name suggests, the shadow interpreters in simple black or white clothing followed closely behind the actors and signed their dialogue. A considerable improvement on platform interpreting – which completely removes the interpreter from the stage action – the shadow technique offered just a glimpse of the theatrical potential of sign and the important role it would soon play in the life of the company.

A few months later, deaf actress Lori Hennessey, and her interpreter Francine Buker, were cast in the musical *Footlight Fantasy* and drew Rod into a new world of sign language.

Rod immediately began lessons, eager to communicate directly with Lori, who was a shy 7th grader. For Fran, whose sign experience was in the regimented and sometimes discouraging world of public school interpreting, the new environment was enchanting. "It seemed very progressive, and it was the most wonderful feeling in the world – to be on stage using my sign," Fran says. Her forthright style as an actress emerged, and her relationship with Access Theatre would continue for nearly ten years.

Fran and Lori's innocence of the theater and Rod's inexperience with sign provoked an enthusiastic, often spontaneous collaboration. "We found a way to be poignant if the scene

"...a sort of garden goddess," wrote Los Angeles *Drama-Logue* critic Susan Stewart Potter of interpreter Kathryn Voice *(left)* in *At Long Last Leo*. "She starts the action and finishes it, and somehow everything seems in her control and strangely blessed because of it."

was poignant, funny if it was funny," Fran recalls, "If something funny happened by accident in rehearsals we kept it." And so when Rod's fingers froze on the expression "yellow bellied, lily-livered sapsucker," and rehearsal came to a halt, the moment was left in so the audience could later share in the joke.

When Michael Douglas sent Rod to visit the National Theatre of the Deaf in residence at the Eugene O'Neill Theater later that summer, Rod saw sign language at work, literally in the hands of professionals. He returned home with a head full of ideas for *Signing Off*, a sign language revue. Casting for this show brought two more deaf actors into the company – six-year old Solomon Smaniotto and Evilio "Victor" Torres, whose stage presence enlivened Access productions through 1987. An American and Mexican sign language speaker, and a dynamic member of the local deaf community, Victor also influenced and educated the company in deaf culture, politics and slang, and helped build visual excitement and content for deaf audience members.

At this time City College sign language professor Peter Robertson also joined the company, bringing years of formal study and a fierce commitment to detail to the table. With all these diverse participants, Access Theatre developed a collaborative and dynamic interpreting style. The interpreters were incorporated as characters, actors signed for themselves, and sign was woven into the dialogue and storylines, even into the choreography of musical numbers.

When *Stage Struck* went into rehearsal in 1982, sign language had a firm place in the life of the company. A new sign language – dubbed RSL (for Rod Sign Language) – enlivened rehearsals as Rod improvised his own sign language shorthand.

Stage Struck brought a new challenge – a large cast, many with no sign experience or with physical disabilities that prevented them from signing. Interpreters Fran and Peter had never worked harder.

"You're interpreting for 35 people all talking to each other, telling jokes, asking questions," Fran recalls. "Even when Rod says 'OK we're taking a break' it doesn't mean your interpreting is over. If you go have a soda with Lori and everybody's chatting, you don't want to exclude her, so you keep on signing. It was hard and thrilling at the same time. Sometimes you just had to say to someone 'wait!' while you tried to catch up, because everybody needed to talk – lighting people, directors, conductors, choreographers. It was really hard coming home and falling asleep. I was always really buzzed."

Backstage, even hearing crew members began to use sign among themselves; their gestures were incorporated on stage and off to cue deaf performers to the music, dialogue, and scenery changes. On stage, the result was powerful for both deaf and hearing audiences because Fran and Peter were blended directly into the show as costumed characters. "*Stage Struck* was very, very difficult because there was a big cast and a lot of words, but it was exciting to watch," Fran says. "We made it as accessible as it could be with a huge cast that didn't sign. We got as close as possible to direct communication as we could – right on top of the actors – practically in their laps. Two characters are screaming at each other and there's the interpreter screaming right back."

—·—

"I loved the way Peter and Fran were incorporated, they were part of everything, and were acknowledged on stage by the actors. It took away that uncomfortable feeling as an audience member when you want to say to the character 'hey, don't you know there's a guy over there on your left?' says Kathryn Voice who joined Access Theatre for the second production of *Stage Struck* in 1983. A beginning sign student and opera singer, she applied her formidable discipline and intelligence to her sign and performance. Over the next 12 years, she made a powerful mark on Access Theatre productions, while also becoming an interpreter and advocate on the staff of the Independent Living Resource Center.

"When I started it was really hard for me to be comfortable speaking English and signing ASL at the same time," Katie says. "I remember how uncontrolled and goofy my voice sounded, it just never sounded real. And I've seen actor after actor go through the same thing. You can see this glazed look come over their faces like 'oh now the hard part.' It's funny to look back on how hard it was, because it seems so natural now."

For each of the company's productions, sign language was essentially a second script. The interpreters poured over the possibilities, and took input from cast members and deaf consultants who sat in on rehearsals. Each translation was a series of sign choices designed to reveal character, move the action,

Rehearsal, *Stage Struck* 1983.

"I always felt connected to her on stage," Remi Sandri says of deaf co-star Lori Hennessey. "There's that little bit of a crush that you have when you don't speak the same language — you're looking very carefully at her face and her eyes, you're really watching. When you're trying to overcome a language barrier there's a lot of give and take that way, there's ultimately a lot of trust that develops."

Music was often central to Access Theatre productions, and deaf actors performed in solo numbers or alongside hearing castmates. Many deaf audience members enjoyed the dance-like interpretations; for others it was the least interesting part of the productions. In *Flavia and the Dream Maker*, interpreter Michael Purcell *(left)* was written into the play as a character and his sign interpretation of the lyrics was blended with Dan Mojica's choreography.

and most importantly convey the show clearly to the deaf audience members. Every production was evaluated for its power to involve both deaf and hearing audiences.

Interpreters also had to be incorporated into the blocking. They had to stay in the light, blend into the stage action, and "toss the visual ball" among themselves in a way that allowed deaf audience members to comfortably follow the dialogue. "With your body and your gaze you direct the focus to the next place it has to be to follow the story," Katie says. "In order to do that there are several steps. You index with your finger to indicate who is talking, get across what they're saying, then toss the visual ball to the next interpreter, who might be interpreting another actor on the other side of the stage. At the same time there's all the stage action the actors are doing, so our philosophy is often less is more. And lots of times ASL turns out to be the more economical use of time to get an idea across.

"One of the strengths and the real beauty and richness of ASL is so many times you can get a crisply articulated idea across and you don't have to do a whole lot of business," Katie continues. "In ASL one of the most important things is body language, what your face is doing, what your posture is doing. It works beautifully on stage because with very small movements you can indicate things with the flick of an eye or a shift of your shoulders, without taking focus away from the actors.

"I've learned you can playfully get an idea across in a very iconic, powerful way that allows the deaf person to catch the meaning, hopefully laugh as close as possible in time with your hearing audience, and then go back to watching the actors. Their eyes don't have to be on the interpreters the whole time, so they get a more complete experience of the performance and a deep feeling of ensemble from the actors.

"But you will not convince every hearing actor that it's a good idea. We've had some ugly scenes, and there were some tough nuts to crack," Katie admits. "One leading actress just walked out; we found her in her car in the parking lot. 'It's just horrible,' she said and she mimicked my gestures, 'it doesn't belong in this show.' In her mind my signing drew every bit of focus there was, and drew the audience completely away from the performances. Another actor kept pushing the interpreter farther and farther out of the light, farther and farther away from him. That had an interesting

"It was exciting to be using sign in an environment that said 'there are no limits, find the best way to communicate.' Sometimes you just wanted to turn a loudspeaker on to the world and say 'hear this! This is important' — because the work and the language came out of camaraderie, collaboration, flexibility, and all the nicer qualities of good people."
Peter Robertson, an ASL teacher and interpreter, was sign language consultant and co-translator on eight of Access Theatre's scripts, and appeared in five of the company's shows between 1981 and 1988.

Rehearsal, *Stage Struck*, 1982.

backlash. The deaf audience members could no longer see both the interpreter and the actor, so they had to watch the interpreter the whole time and they completely missed the actor's performance."

— · —

In 1987, for *Legend of the Crystal Waters*, Rod decided to take the integrated deaf and hearing world he was working with and put it on the stage in a fanciful way. Even the set for *Legend* was designed to sign via flower puppets, vines, and rocks. Playwright Doug Haverty invented three languages for the mythical world – mouthspeak (speech), limbspeak (sign language) and mindspeak, a kind of telepathy. Theatrically, the effect of mindspeak was achieved in several ways. Taped voices spoke and sang for characters who did not use vocal speech, and for all characters when they were communicating via mindspeak. The languages blended naturally into the stage action; lots of costumes and special effects further insured that the musical would remain visually interesting to deaf audiences. Behind the scenes, the ensemble developed a code of signs and subtle cues between hearing and deaf actors – a kind of mindspeak of their own – to integrate

the backstage action for the complex show.

Like *Legend*, most of the Access Theatre productions were original, so sign language and other visual elements were incorporated as part of the creative process. The writers didn't use "hearing jokes" or idiomatic expressions that would be meaningless to non-English speakers. For example, "cat out of the bag," is an English expression – an ASL speaker may simply wonder what the cat was doing in the bag. For the songs, lyricists tried to avoid repetitive phrases, which are boring in sign language, and instead wrote elaborate and plot-driving lyrics that would be more interesting in sign language and in the absence of music.

For Access Theatre's productions of existing plays, the interpreters had a different challenge – to remain true to the playwright's text, while making the play accessible to deaf audience members.

The first of these efforts was the company's production of Mark Medoff's *Children of a Lesser God*. Although the play tells a love story between a deaf student and her speech therapist at a school for the deaf, it was primarily aimed at hearing audiences. Ironically, *Children* had an accessibility problem. The scenes between hearing characters

For Tom Griffin's play *The Boys Next Door,* interpreters
Kathryn Voice *(left)* and Francine Buker covered a
rambunctious cast of 11 characters, and a script full of
hearing puns, foreign words, and idiomatic expressions.
They created their translation with help from deaf audience
members, friends in the deaf community, and interpreting
peers. The result was virtuoso teamwork, well received by
most deaf audience members. Even so, a few more literary-
minded, English-fluent deaf audience members criticized
the choice to use the conceptual-based ASL because it did
not interpret the exact words of the playwright.

In *Storm Reading*, Kathryn
Voice created her most poetic
interpretation for the vignette
of a woman living with a head
injury. It was full of abstracted
signs, inspired by her study
of the great sign storytellers
who create gestural pictures
that are understandable even
for those who do not sign.

Access Theatre's non-human characters
used sign language in ingenious and often
comical ways. The Blob *(above)* signs its
lines in *Finger Talk*; interpreter Peter
Robertson signs as Abra the talking
mountain in the fantasy musical *Legend of
the Crystal Waters (right)*.

were usually only voiced – no sign language. Rod and Peter Robertson added interpreters to fill in where characters did not sign for themselves. The result left local reviewers split – "distracting" wrote one; "beautiful, like an extended piece of choreography," said another, who named the production 'best of 1985.'"

Another difficulty in interpreting established plays is satisfying a diverse deaf audience. Interpretations, like every aspect of theater, are subjectively made, and every choice does not suit every audience member. Some audience members may be interested in seeing the playwright's words signed in exact English, while others may prefer to see the pure ASL interpretation.

"The best situation would be to know exactly who your audience is, but obviously that's not practical," Katie says. "In my everyday interpreting job, I know who my audience is. It's my obligation – my ethical code demands – that I find their language of comfort. As the job goes on, my clients will often send me signs to indicate their preferences.

"But as a performer, we have to make those choices for our audience. And no matter how much feedback we get I know we will not please everybody." As part of an international touring company, Katie has also discovered that regional dialectic differences are as common in ASL as they are in English. "Do you say 'skillet' or 'frying pan'? The same thing happens with sign," she says.

"And sometimes you are going to get hit with something that just won't translate." Katie adds. "I remember in our production of *Twice Blessed*, Fran and I sat in the audience watching Jo Black try to interpret Art Metrano who used a lot of puns and plays on words. And Art ad libs 'He was in a coma, a Perry Coma.' I'll never forget the look on Jo's face. It was such a simple little gag, and the hearing people were laughing hysterically. But even if a deaf person knows who Perry Como – a singer – is, they may not know the English word 'coma,' though they know the sign for the concept. So what are you going to do – sign that this is funny because this singer's last name sounds the same as the English word, only you have to change the last letter…? You would need several minutes of business to explain it all and in the end it would still not be funny. To this day that's our example for 'welcome to the gates of interpreting hell.'"

Over the years, Access Theatre began to develop the visual language of their productions in ever more creative ways, often combining sign with other visual effects. For *Storm Reading*, the company's best-known work, Rod chose to project slides of text in some of the scenes, and lighting and blocking kept things lively visually.

Katie's style and expressiveness as an interpreter/actor peaked with her work on *Storm Reading*. The play, based on the philosophical writings of actor Neil Marcus, gave her the chance to create her most avant garde and individual sign language performance. "At times the interpretation was extremely dance-like and poetic and the sign can become quite impressionistic," Katie says. "The concept is still there, but it's extremely visual and understandable even if you don't sign. Bernard Bragg, a founding member of National Theatre of the Deaf, put a word to this style. He called it the 'visual vernacular.' You have almost blown the words away and gone straight to the concept."

———

"Finding a sign or a gesture that really communicates is a thrill," says Michael Purcell, who joined the company in 1991 for the production of *Flavia and the Dream*

Maker. "The same joy the writer had in choosing the words to communicate the tone and feeling and meaning, it's the same joy you have when you're translating. You're saying to yourself: how will I communicate this thought and make it clear, artistic, surprising?"

Michael was a veteran dancer and actor who had taken up interpreting as his "day job" – his sign was infused with the energy, slang, and street smarts of the Los Angeles deaf community where he often worked and had many friends.

The *Flavia* cast included deaf comedian C.J. Jones and deaf actress Fran Ripplinger, as well as four hearing actors. The small cast all signed, or learned sign, and developed close bonds in the shared language. "Working with deaf performers you have to earn respect for your translations and demonstrate that your choices are good and clear and can work," says Michael, whose empathetic style of signing was perfect for the heartfelt *Flavia*.

"I personally believe no true communication happens between human beings without emotion. It is impossible to do a monologue or a scene or story in ASL without facial expressions, and facial expressions are a result of emotion. With ASL, it's very hard not to communicate your true feelings because people will read you. It's a rich, rich language. I've seen it really bring actors to life, I've seen it bring whole productions to life."

In the years after *Flavia*, Michael worked with Access Theatre's youth program creating translations for four productions and initiating the sometimes reluctant young actors into the world of sign.

For Jaehn Clare's one-woman show, *Belle's On Wheels*, Michael built a translation that relied on visual storytelling, almost pantomime, as well as traditional sign vocabulary. "There were a lot of opportunities for me to suggest the characters she was talking about in her monologues. For example, when she spoke of a lover who left her, I signed the basic information and then I turned out of the scene before it ended, leaving the audience with an image of a man's back and her left alone on the stage. The meaning was self-evident, it didn't need to be spelled out in sign."

"The translation process revealed things to me about my own text," Jaehn says. "And Michael's physicality encouraged me to use more physicality myself. We would often find ourselves unconsciously mirroring each other. For me, the addition of Michael made it a richer performance experience. I felt more engaged, more involved. Going back to doing it without him, I missed the interactive energy between myself and another mind, another body, and another heart."

"As an Access Theatre interpreter, I've never heard the feedback 'I couldn't enjoy the show because that guy was always there waving his arms around,'" Michael concludes. "It's because the interpretation isn't just stuck on as an afterthought. I think that one of Access' strengths was they never tried to separate or ignore the language. It was central to the work, it was going to be there, so we could be open to all its possibilities. Rod regards the interpreter as a fellow artist and he makes that clear by listening and communicating throughout the artistic process.

"I was never just an interpreter at Access Theatre. I've always been an actor, interpreter, human being in some order."

Michael Purcell and Jaehn Clare

Belle's On Wheels, Center Stage Theater, 1995.

"It's almost like putting an amplifier on the actor's
expression, so if they're angry or in love, or whatever
they're feeling, it's supported with the emotions and energy
of another person, and another language," says Michael
Purcell. "People say to me 'your expressions matched the
actor so well.' I never come out front and watch what the
actor's doing facially and copy it. It's because as interpreters
we lock into the same emotions as the actor. We feel what
they feel and put it across with just slightly less energy so
it's always clear that they are the primary characters."

Leslie Johnson and Robin Fortyune, *Kites*, Lobero Theatre, 1984

"I've been training my arms and legs for eons, and sometimes you don't realize what creates powerful expression on stage. He'd just lift his chin, or smile, or turn and face me, and he could be more expressive than any kind of stylized movement that I had learned to do."

Robin and Leslie **pas de deux**

"One of the experiences of being involved in theater is that you achieve daring. It teaches you to leap in darkness. It teaches you to leap in faith, to strive, to stand up and say 'let me, let me.'"

Robin Fortyune, *company member,* Kites

At the Valerie Huston Dance Theatre, the floors were covered in an expensive dancer-friendly linoleum and Valerie was strict about the "no street shoes" rule. She didn't usually have to wonder if wheelchairs would mark up the soft gray floors. She pounded her familiar cane, the one that could coax the passion out of a reluctant student or gutless ballerina, and counted out loud. "And sweep, two, three, four and hold, draw it out...yes!"

The duet was going well. Her rolling cavalier was certainly fearless and the long, dark skid marks told the story – the dance was moving. Even better, between the two dancers

was that intangible chemistry that every *pas de deux* requires, the thing that is or isn't, the thing that can't be choreographed.

Robin Fortyune wasn't sweating but he wished he was, because this was hard work and the studio was hot. Another by-product of his particular quadriplegia, his body thermostat was shot. He stole a look in the mirror, grinned at the determined choreographer and almost missed Leslie Johnson as she swooned gracefully into his arms.

The dance was a central part of Access Theatre's newest work, *Kites*, a unique collaboration between Huston's professional dancers and the Access actors. The two companies met in 1983 when Access Theatre borrowed Valerie's studio for *Finger Talk* rehearsals. Later that year, Rod and Valerie began working on an original musical that would blend the talents of their performers.

In some ways it was the ultimate integration. The dancers were deeply involved with movement; the Access players, who included one physically disabled and two deaf performers, were in more practical ways very physical themselves. The roll of the wheelchair, the articulation of American Sign Language, the visual impact of dance – in Rod's mind it would all fit together.

The result was a whimsical performance art piece, a Sunday in the park with kites, that flowed along on a tide of composer Mark Henderson's lovely melodies. The gentle images left a powerful impression on the audience, and the process taught the players some unexpected lessons about making art.

— · —

Robin Fortyune found Access Theater – as many people did – through Marty Kinrose, who frequently recruited from the driver's seat of the EZ-lift van service. Robin was living on his own in Santa Barbara, attending the University of California. He was four years into his life with quadriplegia, the result of an unspectacular low-speed slip from a dirt bike on the family ranch.

The day of his accident Robin was 17, a "thrill-loving, cow chasing, rabbit-shooting,

country boy" who preferred minor mischief to the boredom of rural California. He had never seen a person in a wheelchair. His life changed when, on a routine chore, his bike slid into a shallow ditch at about 5 mph. Robin's neck broke at the fifth cervical vertebra.

Robin endured a year of grueling physical therapy, thrown not only by his injury but by the breathtaking financial toll on his family. Just before Christmas 1981, he left the hospital for the harsh experience of a seedy halfway house. By June he was living on his own in Santa Barbara, working toward the law degree that would soothe his financial fears and help pay for his mobility and independence.

Access Theatre was a whim, a break from the real world and the constant demands of Robin's post-injury life and education. "I was totally inexperienced in theater, I had no clue," he remembers of the auditions. "But I felt for just a split second when I talked to Rod that there was an opportunity there to experience something in life. And my instinct was 'we'll give this guy a run for his money.'

"I'm afraid I was kind of a difficult son when it came to the rehearsals. I was always a little late, and I didn't take them as seriously as

Diane Reddy, *Kites*, Lobero Theatre, 1984

Rod wanted me to. I'd say 'oh relax, it's a play.' I didn't really get any of this. I was not an artist, I was not emotionally sensitive, I was not inspirational. I was not anything like that. But it kept getting bigger and bigger, and then the orchestra was there, and the audience, and something started happening to me, something completely unexpected."

—·—

Like most original Access Theatre shows, *Kites* evolved throughout the rehearsal process. Composer Mark Henderson and lyricist Eddie Glickman refined the music and songs over several months. Valerie, Rod, and Peter McCorkle developed the dances and storylines into a montage of people who met in the park to picnic, fly their kites, reflect on their lives, and fall in love.

Robin and Leslie's duet was one of nine dances and songs that combined wheelchair movement, dance, and pantomime. Robin's years of stubborn refusal to use an electric wheelchair paid off in rehearsal. "I'm so paralyzed I can barely do the wheelchair, but we used what I knew how to do. It wasn't an accommodation like 'let's get the gimp involved,' it was an *origination*. It was an orig-

inal way of thinking and it worked."

"Valerie wasn't afraid to try things, and Robin certainly wasn't," Leslie says. "It was very spontaneous and new to him. He was still trying to figure out 'what is this body I have?' It was only four years old really, and at that time he was exploring its possibilities.

"To tell you the truth, he was less limited than some trained dancers, because he didn't strike the pose and then kind of figure out what it meant. Everything he did had a natural meaning to it. His sense of form and line went with what he was feeling. A lot of times dancers never learn that, or only learn it when they are very mature.

"As a partner he was wonderful. He wasn't nervous if he could do it or not – he didn't know if he could do it or not. But he was going to do his best and express himself. No dance has ever felt that real for me, with the romance. Ballerinas and their partners always talk about how at the time they're dancing together they're really in love with one another. I was never able to let go and feel that. But in that *pas de deux* I totally forgot that we weren't a couple at that moment. At that moment it seemed perfectly real."

"It was a very intimate and particular

"They had a sense of really being themselves on stage," Robin Ferry says. "Dance is so much about being somebody or something else, it's so much about perfection. It was very, very refreshing to me to see that it was OK, that it was actually *called* for, to be myself. You mean I don't have to be other worldly or something else to be accepted? I don't have to be perfect? I just loved the humanness and the damn *heart* of it. That's what Rod does really well, makes people comfortable with their humanness."

In January and February of 1985, more than 6,000 schoolchildren were bussed in from all over the county to special matinee performances of *Kites*, a city and county school district project made possible by the Lobero Foundation and the California Arts Council.

After the performance, *Kites*, Lobero Theatre, 1985

Robin Ferry *(top right)* and cast *Kites*, Lobero Theatre, 1984

Peter Robertson *(as kite)*

and cast, *Kites*, Lobero Theatre, 1984

"A powerful, zesty evening
of theater...one of the most
entertaining and affecting
shows I've seen in a long
time. It really soared."

Santa Barbara News-Press

Soloist Robin Fortyune and Valerie Huston Dance Theatre, *Kites*, 1984

experience," Robin says, "When I held her in my arms she'd tremble a little, I think that was just her way. It's not like I could protect her. But she felt safe with me. That surprised me. I always thought a romantic hero should be able to defend his castle."

—·—

Every day, the two companies warmed up together at the barre. "We knew we weren't going to become Barishnikovs, but we tried," Katie Voice says. As her spirited renditions of Talking Heads songs rang through the dressing rooms before each performance, the mute dancers gradually began to use their voices with more conviction. "They brought their strengths, we brought ours," Leslie recalls, and they found a common ground in the highly visual *Kites*.

It was not such an odd match. Access company member Peter McCorkle was also a dancer; deaf actor Victor Torres was a native ASL speaker with a theatrical stage presence. Interpreters Katie, Fran Buker, and Peter Robertson were used to expressing themselves physically if not in dance. Young Solomon Smaniotto was a natural, hooked on the music he couldn't hear, but could feel through the stage floor.

"The strength of Access Theatre was the strength of the individual," Leslie remembers, "and they were such individuals. I think they were a little horrified by the way we dancers worked, watching us rehearse and snap to the beat, like a military unit. They were pleased with the result, but the process was not really their style. For them, each person was there because they had a story to tell. They seemed to share a vision for why they were in theater. It was something besides aesthetic perfection or achievement.

"It was an extremely moving experience to be in that show," Leslie adds. "Sometimes as an artist, everything gets ground down to always trying to get somewhere else – like what can this production lead to, how can it make me stronger, or better prepare me to get where I *really* want to go? It's easy to get overwhelmed and lose sight of what we're doing. *Kites* was an end in itself. It wasn't going to turn me into an actress. It wasn't going to do anything for me except to remind me of how openhearted theater can be between you and the audience, and among the whole company, among one another."

Cast, *Kites*, Lobero Theatre, 1984

"As dancers we had a kind of stoicism. And we felt grateful to have a sense of heart again. They were full of ideas and experience, and full of a sense that what they were doing was worthwhile. And it spilled over to us, and stayed with me even after *Kites*. I felt like, I'm going to hold on to this, and never forget that I'm here to be *uplifted*. It was like a transfusion for the spirit, and I didn't even know I needed one."

Leslie Johnson, *Kites*, Lobero Theatre, 1984

"Rod is like a Pied Piper," Robin says. "He throws all your defenses and excuses and stuff out the window and kind of digs down inside for something you didn't even know was there.

"It's genuine 100% belief in an individual, and in people who are physically challenged. It's *because* of their disability. Not because of their difficult station in life, but because they have to exert tremendous mental willingness and energy to deal with their physical abilities. I think he says to himself 'that's a resource, it's not a tragedy, it's a *resource*.' He embellishes upon a person's grit and initiative and he transfers that intensity to a theatrical result. He puts that energy to work.

"Gradually I felt different. When one becomes paralyzed, at least this is how it's been for me, it's like life goes on but you're living it from behind a glass window, and you can see and hear and feel everything, but there's a barrier there that dulls the experience. I was participating in the show, but at first I was just tolerating the whole thing, because I don't believe in quitting. That's how life was for me as a paralyzed individual. Like it's the contender's race at this point. I'm just being frank.

"But something snuck up on me that I did not realize was happening, a kind of magical, child-like bliss that I don't think I could have experienced any other way. It made me really excited to be alive, to have been reckless enough, or daring enough, or stupid enough to participate in the play. And it dramatically broadened my vision of life. It made the window go away. Even though the window's back.

"But for those few minutes on stage, for those minutes when I was actually producing something valuable – which is entertainment – when the music was playing and the auditorium was full, there's a warmth in there, and I was participating in something worthwhile. I wasn't just a spare in life that they'd managed to put together and keep alive. People were there to enjoy who I was."

"The most spectacular thing I learned at Access Theatre is that someone saw something in me that I really did not know was there. And I'm a guy who knows himself pretty damn well. Now whether there is something in me or not, I don't know and I don't care. The result was the same. It made me a greater believer in myself than I was before."

"It gives you an enchanted feeling to have been in that theater," Robin says, "something totally unlike everyday experience. Now that I'm back in the real world, the feeling lingers, to be conjured up unexpectedly. And I think — 'I did that, that was *me*.' I've never been, I've never felt, quite the same since."

Robin Fortyune with Leslie Johnson
Kites, Lobero Theatre, 1984

Tamara Turner as Cora the landlocked mermaid with Remi Sandri

Legend of the Crystal Waters, Oxnard Civic Auditorium, 1985

"Actors are constantly being reborn. I was a veteran actress, but a first time disabled actress. For a lot of people, we feel like we're reborn when we're disabled. We're totally relearning everything – physically, mentally, and emotionally – and developing relationships with the same people in a different way, or losing relationships. I was eight years into my injury when I played Cora, so in some ways I was only eight years old. I was being transformed into a different person."

a mermaid's tale

On March 7, 1979, at a training session in San Luis Obispo, California, 17-year-old gymnast Tamara Turner miscalculated a front somersault on the vault and went headfirst into the mat. She was her team's outstanding athlete and surprised her doctors by regaining the use of some back, chest, and arm muscles. But with her neck broken at the C5-6 vertebrae, she was now living with quadriplegia, dealing with a new body and a new life.

At the time of her injury, Tamara was already a seven-year stage veteran, a regular member of a highly regarded regional repertory theater – "one of the family," she wryly recalls. Though she hoped to continue performing, company management was skeptical. "You'll stand out too much in a wheelchair, it's distracting," she remembers being told. She was out of the family.

Tamara felt betrayed. But she still wanted to act – that, of everything, remained unchanged. She continued to study, and in 1984 a young actor in her singing class, Access veteran Remi Sandri, tried to persuade her that Access Theatre was the right outlet for her talents. She didn't agree.

"I didn't want to do crippled theater," Tamara says now. "I was kind of in denial anyway about myself as a person with a disability. And I wasn't going to go up on stage and be part of people feeling sorry for a bunch of gimps. I wanted to work with talented people, real actors."

At the same time she wondered, "why was this tall, good-looking guy telling me about this theater? He had done leads in two of their productions, he was talented." Her mind churned over the possibilities and the outline of a new dream began to take shape.

Tamara traveled to Santa Barbara, auditioned for Rod – and waited. Unlike the repertory company she was used to, with its five-show season, Access Theatre kept a longer timetable: just one big show a year, usually developed through a long workshop process. Tamara moved to Santa Barbara to be closer to the company. She took the workshops. When producers called Access Theatre looking for an actress, she was cast in a Disney Sunday Movie. And she waited some more.

"Every now and then," Tamara remembers, "Rod would come up to me and look at my wheelchair and say, 'can you push this way, can you push that way, what do you need to sit up?' And I'd say 'why, Rod?' I was dying to be told 'we're doing a show and you've got a part.' But he'd just say 'Oh no reason' and smile the Rod smile."

It was another nine months before Tamara made her re-debut as a stage actress, as Cora the land-locked mermaid in Access Theatre's *Legend of the Crystal Waters*. On February 17, 1987, nearly eight years after her accident, her stage career was on again. It soon took her out of the Access Theatre fold, on a difficult path that peaked at two of the country's great theaters – Washington's Kennedy Center and the Mark Taper Forum in Los Angeles. As it would turn out, Tamara's loud-mouthed mermaid was the beginning of her second chance.

Legend of the Crystal Waters was one of Access Theatre's most seamless integrations of actors with and without disabilities, a fairytale about drought and heros conveyed in a world of costumes, scenic elements, and special effects. Rod came up with the idea during a lecture trip to Japan in 1986; sitting in Tokyo's Noh and Kabuki theaters, he pictured an accessible fantasy musical – though he never imagined how complicated that dream would become.

Back home, he told playwright Doug Haverty that he wanted a "quest," a "fable," something very visual with villains and heros and lots of magic and glowing crystals. Something with a message. Doug, an award-winning author of serious contemporary plays, was keen to try something different. "I was thrilled with the idea of creating this entire world," he recalls. "I really got into it. I'd say 'Rod can I have a waterfall? Can we have somebody disappear into the waterfall? Can we have a talking mountain?' And if Rod said yes, you could be sure it would happen. He loves to accept a challenge."

It took almost nine months to conceive,

Romantic leads Remi Sandri and Lori Hennessey, "Fountains of Hope,"
Legend of the Crystal Waters, Barnsdall Art Park, Los Angeles, 1985

write, and compose the musical. It had the most elaborate set and special effects Access Theatre had ever used, including, as promised, the talking mountain with the waterfall, built by volunteers in Rod's driveway under the supervision of Los Angeles designer and puppeteer Erica Zaffarano.

Legend's experienced cast was small and multi-lingual; the ensemble included two deaf actors, three sign language interpreters, and three hearing actors who signed. Even the mountain – called Abra – was designed to sign. "I wanted to try to create a world where signing was natural, like breathing," Doug says. "Everybody signed, it was second nature." So in *Legend*'s mythical world, the characters spoke three languages: mouthspeak (speech), limbspeak (sign language) and the ultimate communication of mindspeak, a kind of telepathy rendered by means of taped voices. "We wanted to put everyone on a common ground and suggest that maybe speaking with your mouth is kind of primitive compared with speaking with your mind. We wanted the audience to think differently about language and not be able to tell who was deaf and who was hearing," he says.

Doug also created the characters based

directly on the personalities of the actors.

"There are different degrees of magicalness and charm in all of these characters, and it was thrilling to write for these individual actors. Before I started, I sat in a room and talked with each of them one by one. They told me about their lives, likes, dislikes, challenges. We tried to tailor-make the play to them because they were all such vivid people, such a wide range of personalities, each with their own set of complicated virtues."

—·—

"In rehearsal we did a lot of theater games and improv," Tamara recalls. "I'd want to say 'just give me the script.' But the exercises helped me open up – that's probably the most important thing – as a person and as an actor. I took risks, I let go of my inhibitions because I had to. That got me off my little high horse. I found out there were many things I could learn as an actress and there were things inside of me that I didn't need the script for, that I could find through improv.

"It's the most difficult thing to be powerful and project from a sitting position," Tamara continues. "Especially for that character – Cora's loud the whole time," Rod pushed

Exeter (Dave McKay) contemplates the Evil Mortegrim's
stash of precious water. *Legend of the Crystal Waters*,
Lobero Theatre, 1985

In 1986, the Ventura County Office of Emergency
Services commissioned Access Theatre to create a
40-minute video on earthquake preparedness for
deaf citizens. *Silent Quake* starred deaf actors Lori
Hennessey and Larry Littleton and hearing actors
Peter M. Robertson and Millie Brother. Written and
directed by Michael Hughs, with sign language
transcription by Peter M. Robertson, the video
demonstrated earthquake preparedness in American
Sign Language, supported with open captioning and
voice. Funded through the State of California and
distributed through the Governor's Office of
Emergency Services and on cable television, it was
the first such service for the over 17 million deaf
and hard of hearing individuals in the United States.
This video helped bring Access Theatre to the
attention of the Media Access Awards, a California
state program to recognize productions, groups, and
individuals who have contributed through the media
to increased exposure and positive awareness of
people with disabilities. Access Theatre and Rod
himself had been nominated a total of three times
in various categories. On October 9th, 1986, at the
Century Plaza Hotel in Los Angeles, with 300 people
in attendance, television producer Steven Boccho
presented the company with the award for
Outstanding Contribution from an Organization.

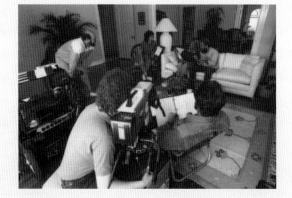

Daniel Hiatt as Gunther. "The lessons and tools which I gathered during my experience with Access Theatre have changed my life," Daniel wrote in a letter to the company, a year into his battle with AIDS, "I have discovered the strength within me to live fully and to make a difference in this world." Access Theatre lost three company members to AIDS: Daniel, *Legend* castmate David McKay, and *Wings* costumer Clifford Olson.

"Is This Any Way to Treat A Mermaid?" Cora (Tamara Turner) and castmates, *Legend of the Crystal Waters*, Lobero Theatre, 1985

hard on the normally soft-spoken Tamara to find the brazen comedienne inside her. "He had to *dig* the loudness out of me, it was a part of me I didn't want to use. Physically it was very difficult too. Like with the breathing, I don't have all the abdominal muscles to support the diaphragm. I was exhausted. I wore an abdominal belt and a strap and I would just grab onto my chair and push my body against that strap. It was a lot of hanging onto my wheelchair and really using the chair and the strap so I could get the force to project. That's what it took to turn Cora on.

"As an actress I'm constantly compromising for loss of tools. One thing I do through the rehearsals is imagine that I am this character and I see myself walking around, physically using every part of my body. If I'm pushing someone away for example, I really see myself pushing this person away, really shoving them down and burying them, and somehow the energy from that develops into the characterization. If I can get that imagination part of it into the character it's an incredible high. If I feel the high I know I'm doing it right. Later a teacher of mine, George Schandoff, spoke of this same technique; he called it 'psychological gestures.' I didn't realize I had been doing it all along.

"Learning to act again has been a learning process on a personal level too. For me, to get through my disability it was usually easier to ignore it. Because sometimes it's just so difficult to accept. The reality of it is so scary if I really sit down and realize what kind of life I'm living, and how society looks at it. So one way to accept it is to ignore it. Like anything painful in anyone's life, you kind of have to deny it and then work through the stages, deny it again, and then work through the stages. When I came to Access Theatre it was hard at first because it brought me out of that denial stage and I had to really look at my disability. Because disability was accepted there, it was OK. I was still like 'no it's not OK, and I'm not disabled.' But after a while I loved it – a world where you're just dealing with people's needs, not pointing out people's differences.

"That's one thing I miss about Access Theater. It's for everybody. You get spoiled. There's audio description, there's sign language, you may even get a good disabled seat when you go to see a performance. When you're in the company you get spoiled too. If there's a difference between any of us, we work it out, we really talk it out. We usually found a way to communicate through the obstacles."

At the Barnsdall Art Park in Los Angeles, the set for *Legend* barely fit into the available space and the crew spent most of the day making it work. As they were finishing up, a group of students who were all both blind and deaf arrived with their interpreters. To prepare themselves for the performance, they came up on stage, felt the set and read a Braille summary of the script.

"I thought I had a pretty open mind," remembers crew member Tal Sanders. "But this time I thought we had just gone too far. And I was so humbled by what happened. The kids were so into it, so entertained." "It was like there was this current between the audience and the actors," adds Doug. "I sat behind them and their fingers were like lightening. They were right there, part of the audience, they didn't stay home and hear about it from an interpreter."

That week in Los Angeles was part of a tour that included two other Southern California engagements, in Palm Springs and at the Oxnard Civic Auditorium, as well as lecture demonstrations to schools throughout the state. Local news and CNN covered the performances. The company won a 1987 California Department of Social Services Director's award and shared the year's Los Angeles Media Access Awards with deaf actress Marlee Matlin, producer Michael Landon, the series *Cagney and Lacey,* and the NBC Nightly News with Tom Brokaw. *Legend* won the American Deaf Drama award for playwright Doug Haverty, and Tamara re-entered the competitive world of professional acting.

———

After *Legend*, Tamara auditioned for and was accepted to the American Academy of Dramatic Arts. She couldn't attend because she couldn't get in the building – there was no ramp. Instead she accepted admission to a professional acting conservatory in Orange County, California. There she appeared as Queen Margaret in *Richard III*, Sue Bayless in *All My Sons,* and Madame Rosemonde in *Dangerous Liasions*, while struggling to educate acting teachers that she could play more than a victim or an old maid.

"The frustration comes when directors see the wheelchair before they see me. Then they just see limitations, and suddenly we're working with all kinds of issues. My disability does mean there are some things that might have to be done differently, but it might not be the things you imagine, and sometimes it might even lead to a better result.

The point is you don't know until you go through the process together. I just want to say, 'let's just start from the acting, let's get past the damn wheelchair.' I don't see this wheelchair all the time, I see *me*, and that's how I go after things and keep up my confidence. But it's a hard barrier to break down. Directors have to worry about money and how an audience is going to perceive things. They may not be particularly creative. They might be limited in their visualization for how a character can develop."

Even so, Tamara's career continued to evolve successfully. She created the role of Brigitte in Nicki Hagenah's original drama *Sweet Chariot*, which debuted in 1989 at the International Very Special Arts Festival at The Kennedy Center. In 1993, she joined an outstanding cast led by actress/director Victoria Ann Lewis to co-write and appear in *PH*reaks* at the Los Angeles Music Center's Mark Taper Forum.

"I still hung onto the fantasy that I was going to be able to make a living as an actress.

I looked at Remi who took his suitcase from theater to theater and I wanted that. But it really was a struggle and it's kind of a vicious circle; you're fighting not to be looked at as 'disabled,' but you're also fighting to have issues about your disability taken into consideration. You end up in the middle a lot."

Tamara fell in love, with a man who had been in the audience of *PH*reaks,* and returned to college full-time to pursue another of her passions, working with children. She gave up the idea of being a theater gypsy, though she continues to act, study, and write.

"I suppose I could say that I was prevented from pursuing an acting career because of my disability," Tamara says, "and that would partly be true. But I am also a part of every choice, and God is always leading me to new places. I finally decided on more balance in my life. Now I want a regular paycheck, I want time for my relationship.

"Acting is a difficult profession, even more so for someone with a disability, and I got tired of pioneering the same stuff over and over again. There's such a tendency to typecast, either as the heroic survivor, or the frumpy, asexual supporting character. But women who have disabilities can be cast as

Mortegrim (Ian Kelly) and Doria (Lori Hennessey),
Legend of the Crystal Waters, Lobero Theatre, 1985

Composer Mark Henderson wrote and performed the score for
Legend on his new MIDI computer system; arranger Dan Slider
(far left) filled the music with rich New Age-style orchestrations
and special effects. With lyricist David Strauss they created
narrative songs, including the ballad "Somewhere" performed
by Kathryn Voice and acknowledged by a local theater critic as
one of the ten highlight performances of 1987. *Legend*'s songs
were presented as a combination of live singing and taped
performances by local musicians including rocker Kenny
Loggins *(left)*, who sang the show's prologue.

"What appealed to me about the show? That for my entrance I would be burped and spit out of a giant mountain. And for my exit I would take the lady's hand and disappear into a waterfall and a cloud of smoke."

Remi Sandri
Legend of the Crystal Waters, Lobero Theatre, 1985

Legend's strong environmental message and water themes inspired a unique collaboration among local water districts, Access Theatre, the Lobero Foundation, Arco, and other local sponsors to bring *Legend* to thousands of school children. Access Theatre's teacher's guide also outlined strategies for communicating with students about disability, environmental, and conservation issues.

106

Tamara with Kareem
Abdul-Jabbar on the
set of the Disney
Sunday Movie *Ask
Max*; in **PH*reaks* at
The Mark Taper Forum;
and meeting Senator
Ted Kennedy after her
debut in *Sweet Chariot*
at the Kennedy Center.

girlfriends, as mothers with children, as career women: we can be fleshed out as characters. So often the wheelchair is substituted for the personality, as if people who use wheelchairs were their *wheelchair*, and not human beings – every *kind* of human being."

—·—

"Opening night of *Legend*, I didn't think I was going to be so nervous," Tamara remembers. "I felt like I was really going to throw up right before I went on stage. I kept wanting Rod to be there the whole time. He's the director and he has a million things to do and I'm like 'Don't leave me!' It was my first time in a wheelchair out on stage, and Cora comes out spittin'. I had to have everything behind it. It went great. Cora is so funny that people were laughing, and I thought 'hmm, people are laughing.' The first two rows were full of friends and family going 'oh my God, look at *her*.' And I knew it was working.

"It gave me that old feeling again. I always feel when I'm doing theater that I'm at home. Sit down in my living room and be a part of my home. I like being on stage, I feel at ease. People can see who you are, and I can feel myself pulling people into me, making those little adjustments as I go along to make sure I'm reaching the audience, building the relationship – like creating family. It's like the audience becomes my family. That's what I love most about acting."

Kathryn Voice, Fran Buker, Dan Hiatt, and Dave McKay with young audience member,
Legend of the Crystal Waters, Barnsdall Art Park, 1985.

Neil Marcus, Kathryn Voice and Roger Marcus, *Storm Reading*, 1988

In March of 1988 a few days before *Storm Reading* opened at the Lobero Theatre, playwright/actor Neil Marcus and Rod Lathim sat in an all-night restaurant eating cake. Neil was saying earnestly "I want the *world* to hear my words," and Rod was thinking "Nice dream Neil."

It's hard to pinpoint the exact moment when the dream came true. Maybe it was when Maria Shriver interviewed Neil on *The Today Show* or when Linda Wertheimer broadcast her interview with him on National Public Radio's "All Things Considered." Maybe it was the night Neil took his bow at the Kennedy Center with Michael Douglas and Lauren Bacall before a national television audience. Maybe it was when *Storm Reading* received its final standing ovation at the Cultural Paralympic Festival in Atlanta. Actually the dream came true little by little, audience by audience – in famous houses such

as Miami's Coconut Grove Playhouse, and in smaller theaters in Alaska, Albuquerque, England, Vermont, and Vancouver. Over the course of eight exhausting, exhilarating years, the world did hear Neil Marcus' words, and they are still heard today, as Neil continues to write and perform, and *Storm Reading* continues its life on video.

It's the kind of success all playwrights hope for. It was all the more surprising that Neil should be one of the few who achieved it. Neil's awkward speech, and body like an unbroken colt, can inspire the man on the street to glaze over or turn away rather than decipher what he has to say. Having said that, if anyone was going to make an international spectacle out of himself it would be Neil, and he had the ammunition to make it work. That ammunition was contained in his diaries and writings, a ten-year collection of wise, funny, biting and empathetic observations about life, specifically his life.

It wasn't just Neil's words that got to people. For many, the real punch of *Storm Reading* came from Neil's appearance on stage as himself – a storyteller like no one had ever seen before. Literally. Night after night, as audiences sat with Neil and his memories, they also experienced him in real time, up on stage. They got a glimpse into his unusual life as it was happening. To their unlimited surprise many, many people saw themselves in Neil's stories and others felt lifelong misconceptions wither away in two hours of staring at him. A lot of people cried when it was over, then stood in line to hug Neil in the lobby after the show. They felt relieved of a burden they didn't know they had and they loved him for it. That's one theory anyway.

Whatever the reason – and there were probably many – *Storm Reading* was to become Access Theatre's most widely seen and successful show. It brought the company international recognition and gave Neil Marcus his debut to the whole wide world. And the world, to its amazement, is very glad to know him.

"His body is curved like a sensuous pretzel," Neil writes of himself, of the body he has been collaborating with since he was eight years old and his dystonia began. Initially, and for many, many months, Neil was told that his body's rebellion was all in his head; to a little boy that meant the terrifying and lonely thought that he was crazy. Psychologists blamed his nervous parents, masturbation, and assorted repressed emotions; they noted with surprise that Neil's symptoms failed to respond to a placebo, indicating that he was hanging on to them rather more tenaciously than expected. Meanwhile his body continued to reinvent itself in scary and inconvenient ways, until finally there was a name for it: *dystonia musculoram deformans*, a rare neurological disorder that causes severe, sometimes continuous, muscle spasms and involuntary jerks. It has no effect on the mind, except maybe to make a person think a little more about things. Neil was relieved to know that he wasn't crazy. But he still had to deal with a million questions about his life, which doctors told him would probably not last into his mid-twenties.

Matthew Ingersoll and Neil Marcus, *Storm Reading*, 1996

Playwright Neil Marcus has flourishing dystonia, a neurological condition which allows him to leap and soar and twist and turn constantly in public, thus challenging stereotypes of every sort and making him very interesting to watch and sit next to during lunch hour. It rides him like a rollercoaster at times. Not much is known about dystonia. Touch, understanding, and attention can be very helpful. Fear and dread are not helpful. The playwright has 'generalized dystonia' which means it is all over him like a phone line that links world nations. It makes Neil very alive, but then again, aren't we all???

Neil Marcus

—·—

Even with his diagnosis, Neil had nothing to conform to, just a desire to live with meaning and style, so he tried different things. He took up skateboarding; he became valedictorian of his high school class; he went off to college in Washington State. He went on a solo journey to Laos; he threw himself onto the steps of the Oakland city hall to protest funding cuts for accessibility programs. He ended up living in Berkeley in an 8th floor apartment with a great view and access to the

legendary Center for Independent Living, the hub of the nation's liberation movement for people with disabilities. There Neil met other non-conformists and began to write voraciously, starting his newsletter *Special Effects* and accumulating the observations and words that would become *Storm Reading*.

Storm Reading began to take shape as a play when Neil's brother Roger, an actor, created a dramatic interpretation of Neil's writing and taped it for Rod.

Roger had a feeling that there was theatrical gold in the diaries Neil pecked out on his word processor, one dystonic finger at a time. Rod saw a mix of insight, frustration, and humor and a Walt Whitman-esque economy of words, that seemed perfect for the stage. "There's no fat on Neil's work," Rod says. "He doesn't have the time or stamina to sit and type with one finger about nonsense. When he speaks it's direct and concise."

Even so, there was a massive amount of raw material that needed to be edited, shaped, and revised. Most of all, the words needed a theatrical context. There had to be a powerful stage picture to match the power of Neil's words. Rod, Neil, and Roger went to work on the adaptation and decided to create a kind of one-man show for three players. Neil would appear as himself, while Roger would be his voice and portray the many characters that populate Neil's life and imagination. Kathryn Voice's artistic sign interpretation was woven into the action and she assumed some of the characters as well.

Over the next months, rehearsals were harder than anyone could have imagined, especially for Neil. As a first-time actor he needed hours of rehearsal, punctuated by breaks – sometimes every few minutes – to rest his body. Tension made his spasms worse; it was nerve wracking to try to hit a mark the same way twice, or coax a line out of his reluctant tongue. Rod worried that Neil might be seen as a prop in his own show. At the same time, Rod could see they were creating something wholly original. Neil's emotions fluctuated from an ecstatic 'we've got a hit on our hands' to this journal entry the following month: "I pulled the set over in rehearsal. The lights are blinding. I can't see. I can't move. I'll never make it."

"Acting on stage is like a giant pinball/ bio-feedback machine," Neil finally concluded. "The goal is to relax and act well." Opening night Neil was so tense, sweaty, and dizzy that he collapsed during intermission. He took a Valium, then went on to finish the show to a standing ovation and the stunned response of critics. "A knock-out," said the *Santa Barbara News-Press*. "Dazzling, profound, ingenious."

Two months later, Access Theatre gambled $13,000 on a one night stand at the Doolittle Theatre in Hollywood. Funded largely by Michael Douglas, screenwriter/ director David Seltzer and producer Gary Goddard, the performance was a showcase for executives at Disney, Warner Bros., Columbia, NBC and others, intended to generate more opportunity for *Storm Reading*. The performance was greeted with a standing ovation, followed by...nothing.

For weeks, Rod and company wondered if they had lost the gamble, when gradually the phone started to ring. Los Angeles based agency Mainstage Management International took the show onto its roster, and secured the first crucial touring engagements. A few more dates trickled in, and then a few more. Each time *Storm Reading* was performed, more bookings came in. Through word of mouth its reputation would continue to spread, until people had seen the show across the country from Honolulu to Portland, Maine.

In June of 1989, the skies over Washington D.C. raged with the worst thunderstorms in 100 years, as Access Theatre arrived in town for the Very Special Arts International Festival. *Storm Reading* would play at the historic Ford's Theatre, where Lincoln was assassinated. The week culminated in a gala performance at the Kennedy Center taped for broadcast as an NBC special "From the Heart." Some 3500 people attended the taping, which featured appearances by festival artists, as well as two dozen stars including Mikhail Baryshnikov, Lauren Bacall, Lou Gossett, Melissa Manchester, Jim Henson, and Kermit the Frog.

Years earlier, long before *Storm Reading* was conceived, Rod had been in Washington and had taken the guided tour of the posh Kennedy Center, never imagining Access Theatre would perform there. "When I walked in and saw the set and the TV cameras, it hit me, we were really there," Rod says. He walked out onto the theater's terrace overlooking the Potomac and took a rare chance to savor the accomplishment.

"It was a very heady time for Rod,"

Kathryn Voice remembers, "for all of us." But Katie points out that the opportunity also came with one of the inevitable drawbacks of television. "There's always a temptation in the media to portray people with disabilities as heroic," she says, "to go for the heartstrings. That element certainly brings in funds and audience, but it's actually a very safe and mediocre view. Rod's been brave enough to say, 'that isn't the vision I hold for this company,' and his conviction was tested at the Kennedy Center," Katie says.

"We were rehearsing with Michael Douglas, who was introducing us on the show," she explains. "At the end, the producers from NBC wanted him to somehow put this warm congratulatory arm around Neil, to milk the moment for all that it was worth. Rod was watching in the audience and I knew he was not going to like this idea. The producers were pretty big names, and I thought 'I wonder if Rod will say something?' And sure enough he came right up on stage and without making a big deal about it, he quietly said, 'we'd like to make another choice.' So Michael just finished his words with his hand by his side, very respectfully. A lot of people might not have known that etiquette-wise it was not appropriate to

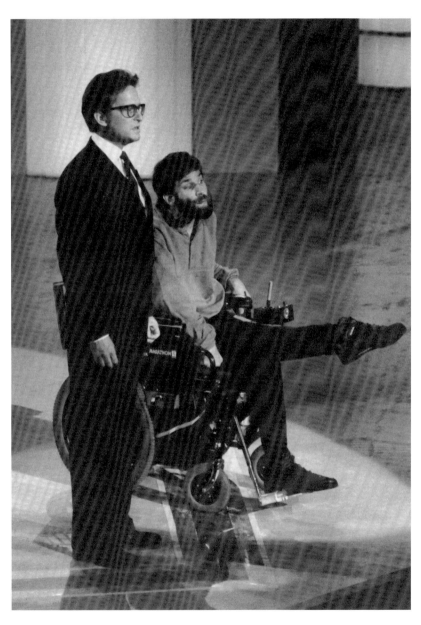

Michael Douglas and Neil Marcus in the NBC television special
From the Heart. The Kennedy Center, 1989

In 1988, filmmakers Anthony Edwards and Shawn Hardin (above with sound man Chick Cashman) shot 22 hours of video on the road with *Storm Reading* in Taos, Albuquerque, Santa Fe, and Colorado Springs. The footage captured the hectic pace of the tour and caught glimpses of the show on stage; Edwards painstakingly edited the tour segments plus a collection of interviews with cast and crew into a half-hour documentary, *Speaking Through Walls*. "I wanted to tell a story that was compelling, that had heart and strength," Edwards says of his first project behind the camera. "I wanted to tell a story I cared about." Edwards presented a rough cut of the documentary at Access Theatre's 10th anniversary gala; the finished film aired at the Santa Barbara International Film Festival. The film went on to win the Council on International Non-Theatrical Events (CINE) Golden Eagle Award and the National Educational Film & Video Festival award.

Sign language interpreter Kathryn Voice was Neil's collaborator
from the first performance; her husband Matthew Ingersoll joined
the cast in 1990. Katie did the final Santa Barbara performances
pregnant with Grey, the couple's first child.

Kathryn Voice, Matthew Ingersoll and Neil Marcus, *Storm Reading* 1996

touch Neil and his wheelchair in that way in a formal setting. So I was glad to not have that inappropriate message be broadcast on national TV. I was glad we got to hold on to our integrity."

During the week in Washington, Linda Werthheimer invited the cast to NPR studios for an interview that aired with excerpts from the show on "All Things Considered." Back in Santa Barbara, the company phones began ringing immediately, as calls came in from people who had heard the radio broadcast and wanted to book *Storm Reading*. Meanwhile back in Washington, Rod and the cast finished a round of press conferences and workshops; at a party on the White House lawn, Neil shook George Bush's hand, man to man.

— • —

When Neil's dream of communicating with the world came true, it was hard on him in unexpected ways. As it turned out, acceptance into society tested his resolve as much as isolation had, maybe more. It was tough on his body and tough on his self-image as an unlimited person. "It was hard to ask for help," remembers Neil, who normally lives alone. "I learned how to get help and hopefully to not

be so scared. I needed more help caring for myself in order to do the play. I had to accept that." And though Neil's stamina and articulation as an actor increased with every performance, most nights it was still a battle on stage.

My shortcomings are being pushed in my face...maybe it's OK to be weak, to stumble, trip or fall onstage. I mean, this play is my life. The event of doing it is really what my life is like. Why shouldn't they see everything? Maybe this is unlike any theater ever before. It's real. Theater might be life. I might be theater.

Neil Marcus, telex to Roger Marcus

Neil kept writing, and inevitably the show kept changing to reflect Neil's new writing and his development as an actor and a person. Rod continuously reevaluated the text, adding things, cutting things, changing blocking, even sets and costumes, as the production evolved. In 1989, Rod realized that it was time for Roger Marcus to leave the show. For two years, the chemistry and strong physical resemblance between the two brothers had been a magical aspect of the show, and Roger had carried the load as the more experienced actor. But consequently the show had come to be

Neil Marcus, Matthew Ingersoll and Kathryn Voice, *Storm Reading*, 1996

dominated by Roger.

"Neil had grown tremendously as an actor," Rod remembers. "It was time for Neil to come into his own as the focus of the play." Rod didn't believe this could happen without changing the show in ways that would not work for Roger. Improvisational artist Matthew Ingersoll replaced Roger and *Storm Reading* was reinvented for its next incarnation.

"I remember the very first time I performed before a live audience in Duluth, Minnesota and it bombed," Matt remembers. "Usually when the audience is quiet Rod says it's because they're listening, but this time they weren't listening. It was a disaster. I thought this is it, this is the end for the play." The "disastrous" performance received a standing ovation. So did the next night's performance at the World Theatre in Minneapolis, best known for Garrison Keillor's broadcasts.

As the new cast continued to work together, Neil blossomed in the spotlight. With Matt's comedy background the show began to lighten up. It also became less predictable, which suited the improv-trained Matt, who used his skills to help keep the play on track as the three actors developed an almost telepathic rapport on stage.

"It makes the play very exciting and very immediate," Matt says. "More real. With Neil, a line may take longer than you think to get out and the momentum of the play might flatten out for a second. Or a mark will be missed, or I'll drop a line, or Katie will, so the air will sometimes get let out of the balloon. But that doesn't have to be a bad thing," Matt says. "Sometimes the suspense is thrilling," Neil adds.

"It gives us a lot of variety," Matt continues, "and we start rebuilding the momentum immediately. Or we take that mistake and use it. It may create an opening for me to say something that will read as funny to the audience. You have to think quickly, in fact it's like what people say about car accidents – that time slows way down. Things would happen every night. Neil's leg would go up and he would hit us. He might end up being in a different place on stage where he isn't supposed to be. He might spit when he talks, so you'll be in the middle of scene and all of a sudden you've got spit on your face. Now do you choose to ignore that or do you acknowledge it? I would choose to acknowledge it, because the audience has seen it happen and that happens in real life.

Lauren Bacall with Neil Marcus, Roger Marcus, Katie Voice, and artists of the
Very Special Arts International Festival. The Kennedy Center, 1989.

Interpreter Michael Purcell, Rod Lathim, and guest host Anthony
Edwards at *Storm Reading's* video taping. Emmy-award winning
director Gary Smith, producer Dann Netter of Smith/Hemion
Productions, and a four-camera crew shot the video over the course
of two evenings and did extensive post production. The video was
produced with $150,000 in grants from the G. Harold and Leila Y.
Mathers Charitable Foundation, the Blanche and Irving Laurie
Foundation, the E.L. Weigand Foundation, the NEC Foundation of
America, and an anonymous angel. The video aired on national cable
television, and 1000 captioned and audio-described tapes were
distributed to schools and non-profit agencies throughout the country.

"With Neil it's always fresh," Matt concludes. "Neil's whole life is improv, and the play is part of his life. I prefer it when it doesn't go the same way every night. Otherwise the play is driving you, and I'd rather we were driving the play. We all looked forward to the little spontaneous moments of magic that make a show worth doing over and over again."

———

Storm Reading traveled successfully off and on through 1996 to twenty states, Canada, and England. It had its Manhattan debut at the Tribeca Arts Center. It played at universities including Stanford and UCLA, and in theaters from Idaho to Ohio to Maine – a broad diversity of towns and venues and an endless variety of conditions.

Backstage, when things got tense, technician Tal Sanders would go into his Bob Dylan imitation; program director Daniel Girard would counter with Beavis and Butthead. "It cracked Rod up and it was kind of a mantra for chilling out," Tal says. Tal, Daniel, company manager Thom Rollerson, and technical directors John Kelly, Ted Dolas, and Kathleen Parsons traveled with *Storm Reading*

over the years, and helped Rod handle the ever-changing demands that go with taking a show on the road. Though *Storm Reading* became a well-oiled machine, there was always the unexpected – broken equipment, lost luggage, and worst of all an electric wheelchair that emerged from baggage claim in pieces more than once.

But most often the unexpected came from the audiences, who always had a strong reaction, usually good. "It's easier to single out the few people who didn't get it," Thom says, "like the guy who thought Neil should be put into bed and spoon fed. Some of the people that came to see Neil's show would have walked out of their way to avoid Neil before they saw the show, and they come up to him afterwards and want to hug him. We witnessed many, many tears and testimonials of personal transformation, sometimes in the most unlikely places."

"In Reno, we pulled up to perform at a Catholic high school that looked like a prison," Rod remembers. "We couldn't figure out how to get in; we were dreading the experience. It was an enormous wooden floor gymnasium, no set, acoustics from hell, uncomfortable bleachers for the audience. An Irish priest led a prayer before the performance. So we prayed

At the core of my being, I have felt that life is a dance.

That my life is a dance. I am a dancer.

I dance.

Knowing this has given me a great sense of pride.

The world says "You are a spastic quadriplegic."

I say I'm a dancer.

There's a new movement happening in the world.

People are beginning to realize they are more

than what they've been told they are.

The flame is fanned.

The fire spreads.

Every moment is a new moment

to do what's never been done before.

From *Storm Reading*

right along with him. We rolled out there onto this big bare, silent space. You could have heard a pin drop. Then the kids caught on and began to laugh, and support, and clap. It was an incredibly elevating experience for all of us. And it just proved we should never prejudge what's going to happen."

In fact, with *Storm Reading*, gambling on an audience was part of the point. In Vancouver, at a performance sponsored by the founders of the Dystonia Medical Research Foundation, Neil took particular satisfaction in performing for a full house of medical professionals – shaking clinical views of dystonia and its limitations with living proof.

When the company appeared at Manchester's Green Room Theatre as part of the United Kingdom's City of Drama Festival, *The Guardian* responded with a review that echoed many other reviews throughout *Storm Reading's* long touring life. "(Neil Marcus) captures the audience defiantly, unsentimentally for two hours of wildly funny, sharp philosophical musing on his – and the human – predicament. It's an astonishing celebration of life. It's an exhilarating, liberating experience." After seeing the opening night of the company's five-week run at the Tiffany

Theatre in West Hollywood, Mike Frym wrote in *Daily Variety*, "An unforgettable perception altering experience...profoundly revitalizes the audience's sense of humanity...placing *Storm Reading* in the 'must see' category."

Everywhere they went, the company used the opportunity to raise awareness of disability issues, giving what seemed like endless workshops, consultations, and press interviews, which often turned into impromptu therapy sessions. "The show got people to stop and think about what they are doing on the planet," Rod says. "To ask, 'am I using my time wisely? Am I communicating? Am I carrying baggage around I don't need?' This show is a great reminder to get over it and live."

"I had been using a peashooter to effect change in the world," Neil says, "with *Storm Reading* I had a shotgun."

Dear Neil,

I came home tonight and I told my parents of your performance. It's not like me to talk sincerely with them very often, but I found myself describing what I saw you and your companions express today. What I saw was absolutely extraordinary. You managed to touch the hearts of over three hundred

Kathryn Voice and Neil Marcus
make a tentative stab at romance.
Storm Reading, 1988.

teenagers, which is no easy accomplishment. You opened many eyes today and revealed to them the incredible power of the human mind and spirit and their ability to overcome adversity. We can all learn so much from what you say and I truly thank you for giving me the opportunity to learn from you. Someday I wish I could be a part of something as worthwhile as what you do.

Frank, October 1994

Dear Neil,

My cousin Daniel has cerebral palsy. After watching you perform I called him up to tell him what I saw and learned from the performance. For the first time I was able to talk with my cousin, without the sense of being uncomfortable or having the fear of saying something that would offend him. I finally talked to Daniel as a cousin instead of a human with cerebral palsy, who I had trouble opening up with. This was one of the greatest feelings of my life and I would like to thank you completely for giving me that experience.

Josh, October 1994

Dear Neil,

Your name reminds me of Neil Armstrong, but you are more handsome! Please read on, this is not a love letter. I had the opportunity to see Storm Reading yesterday. I saw the storm in you, I saw the storm that is you. You are the storm that calmed everything that was disturbed and confused in me. Thanx Neil. Wow!

You taught me that I should stop pretending what I cannot be and start liking what I am. You have given me reason to smile every time

 I go to Burger King

 I travel in a train

 I eat garbanzo beans

 You are so rare Neil, I would have hated going through life without knowing you.

Bhavna, May 1989

———

"I have always maintained that disability is a never-ending struggle to achieve perfection. It is not a brave struggle or courage in the face of adversity…disability is an art. It's an ingenious way to live. Who would ever think of living that way if they weren't disabled?

Neil Marcus

Neil says things in a way that people can understand. Access Theatre's *Storm Reading* presented him in a way that was even clearer and more vivid. Yet, even well-meaning journalists, even those who saw the show, still used words to describe him such as twisted, wracked, dependent, tragic, stricken with incurable dystonia, and confined to a wheelchair. Neil Marcus received critical acclaim in theaters that were inaccessible to him, where he had to be carried up stairs to reach the stage to receive his standing ovation. This is not just ironic, it is reality. But Neil also tries to see it all as an opportunity.

"It takes a great deal of effort not to be overcome by the sheer weight of discouragement and hopelessness that I as a disabled person feel," he writes. "It's scary to be real, to be vulnerable, to admit that I'm not happy all the time. If I can talk to another human being and tell them what's in my heart...it helps, that's meaning for me.

"Our lives, disabled people's lives, provide us, in a unique way, with tools for living. Our lives give us knowledge which can be useful to others. Disabled people﹐hold a powerful store of knowledge about coping with unfavorable and sometimes hostile environments, and creating a sense of self worth beyond one's physical limitations." *Storm*

Reading proves this with an unflinching tour of Neil's life, and closes with a challenge, an invitation to find grace and empathy:

> *When you walk into a room*
> *full of people*
> *and there's a disabled person in the room*
> *and she scares you*
> *or you want to avoid him*
> *or she mystifies you*
> *or you want to reach out and help*
> *but don't know how...*
> *when this happens you are on*
> *the cutting edge of liberation.*
>
> *See a disabled person clearly*
> *and chances are you'll see*
> *yourself clearly.*
> *That is when there are no limits...*
> *And there are no limits as to*
> *when that will happen*
> *It will probably happen...now*
>
> Neil Marcus, *Storm Reading*

In 1991, the United Nations Society of Writers honored Neil Marcus with the Writers Literary Award and a Medal of Excellence. In 1993, Los Angeles' *Drama-Logue* magazine gave *Storm Reading* three awards – for production, ensemble, and direction.

In 1996, after nearly a year of not performing together, the cast reunited to tape two performances at the Lobero Theatre for television and video distribution. Back on the same stage where it debuted, lit for the camera, and supported by an adoring local audience, *Storm Reading* looked mature and polished. Neil was now, unmistakably, an actor, confident in his material and able to play off Matt and Katie with often subtle gestures. It seemed a fitting last performance.

It did not turn out to be the last performance. Seven months later they all traveled to Atlanta to appear in the Cultural Paralympiad Festival, directly following the Atlanta Games, before an international audience of fans. During that same trip, a special performance was filmed for national television as part of the USA Network series "Erase the Hate" (since retitled "It Just Takes One").

"The work that I do with the arts reflects the respect that I feel towards all of life," Neil Marcus says, "I have knowledge that people are good and that I am good. I didn't always know this.

"The message we often get in society that we are worthless, unimportant beings is a lie. We are glorious, essential, intelligent human beings, deserving of absolutely the best from life."

On **stagecraft**

and Accessibility

Backstage at the Lobero Theatre, there are ghosts. Nothing specific, nothing sinister, just the accumulation of history that sticks to the ropes and flys, catwalks and floorboards of a 120-year-old theater. The Lobero has hosted Henry Fonda, Dame Judith Anderson, and the eager minions of countless local dance recitals. Hundreds of sets have been built and struck on the nearly square stage, hundreds of fresnels have expended their lamp hours in the lighting grid and many, many practical jokes have been successfully executed. Mixed in with the spirits of *Our Town* and *Nutcracker*, with the fragments of music, applause, and backstage bickering, are the whispers of ten Access Theatre shows, and the sound of Reg Lathim cursing at a broken fog-making machine half an hour before curtain.

The Lobero was Access Theatre's first stage and it always made the performers feel that they had made the big time. The venerable

setting also created pressure for Rod, who knew that all his productions, from the very first, had to look as professional as possible.

So Rod and company learned how to stretch a dollar until you could practically see through it. They shopped for costumes and props in thrift stores, they recruited volunteers, they improvised. But even though every dime counted, Access Theatre shows were not produced with a sense of making do. They were ingeniously made – to fit the script, the budget, and the accessibility needs of actors and audiences. Every production was a technical adventure, because no matter how much anyone learned on the previous show or tour, there was always a new wrinkle, or a new technology to master, or a new idea that Rod just had to try.

—·—

Most Access Theatre productions were original works, so set, costumes, and technical design were created alongside the script. This collaborative process among the designers and writers allowed the company to be innovative and flexible, developing sets that ranged from minimalist to fanciful to realistic, and adjusting them as the show evolved.

From the start, Rod, who had good design sensibilities himself, chose collaborators who knew about visual art, including local art instructor Susan Warren who worked on the early shows. "He was very interested in the whole stage picture," Susan recalls, "so part of what he expected from me was to look out for that, to make suggestions not just about color or set design, but even about things like composition in how the actors were blocked. He thought all of it was important, and he was open to suggestion on any detail. He creates an environment where people tend to pitch in with their ideas."

They didn't just pitch in with ideas. Local businesses donated lumber, nails, paint, and foam rubber; volunteers donated labor. "I never ceased to be tickled that people would just take on projects," Rod says "Someone would say 'we've got this cool idea for posters.' And they would go off and come back with far more than we ever had in mind."

The father of one of the actresses, Joe Hennessey, masterminded the curved ramps for *Stage Struck's* revolving modular set. "We built it in his garage," Rod remembers, "and out at the Edison power station where he worked. So I would run from rehearsal to Joe's house to my folks' house, where my mom was working on costumes."

As Access Theatre's shows became more and more professional, this collaborative working process remained the model. Lighting and scenic designer Theodore Micheal Dolas, who designed seven of the company's later shows and also served as a technical director on the *Storm Reading* tour, remembers what it was like to start in on a new design. "We'd talk about what kind of feeling the story had – the warm and cold elements, the humor, what the characters were like, where we wanted the audience to be in relationship to the set. We'd have a general meeting and then Rod and I would go away from that and think, and I'd come up with a sketch or a model.

"The first time through we didn't worry about costs," Ted continues. "Then we'd deal with the budget, and try to come up with ways to get the image we wanted within that budget. Sometimes this meant taking wide slashes out

Designer Erica Zaffarano *(above left with Rod)* and dozens of volunteers applied over 2000 square feet of foam and 100 yards of cheesecloth to a modular iron armature to create the magical set for *Legend of the Crystal Waters*. The finished set featured a working waterfall, fog, and dry ice effects, and created the epic fantasy setting Rod had imagined for the show.

of the design. We had to know how to do that and still make it work. Some of the most important details are not about money – for example, I think about color constantly. And Rod is very conscious of color. We have gone together to pick paint – it all costs the same, but the right colors in paint, lighting, and costumes can make or break the look of a show."

For Ted, who envisions how he will light a set right from the beginning of the design process, the power of light to shape a production was also a primary concern. "I threw away a lot of the rules on these shows, sometimes because I didn't have a lot of equipment to work with, sometimes because I just wanted to try something different." His lighting design for *Storm Reading* changed along with the show over the six years of its run, and light was virtually a character in the show. "Lighting can illustrate things like time and character," Ted says, "it can be used to accent an actor's emotion, to make it overt or subtle."

In *Storm Reading*, the person calling the lighting cues was actually collaborating with the actors, because actor Neil Marcus' performance was always a little different, and sometimes unpredictable. "You would judge how to time a cue, or when to black out after a punch

line," Ted says. "You had to be aware of what the audience was feeling, how they were reacting and get into their rhythm.

"Access shows were very demanding. You had to be flexible, you always had to be willing to do what it took for the good of the show. You could not just sit back and say 'I'm the designer and it's got to be this certain way.' I am kind of a perfectionist. I lack the ability to say 'close enough' and let it go, but there are many different ways to get what you want."

———

In the fall of 1986, motorists driving up Chapala Street past Rod's tidy little house had to wonder. What was growing in the driveway? Every weekend, it got bigger, as volunteers clambered on scaffolding and slathered foam, cheesecloth, and latex onto a 27-foot wide by 12-foot tall mountain, the set for *Legend of the Crystal Waters*.

"It amazed me that people were willing to sacrifice so much time," remembers Erica Zaffarano, the Los Angeles scenic artist and puppeteer who designed the set. "People just jumped in, especially Rod's parents. They were either bringing food or they were handling the latex. Kathy Lathim had a lot of latex on her all the time, I remember. She was a little worried at first that she wasn't doing things right, and then she started to blossom. She realized there was no way to do anything wrong, that we were going for texture and the more 'mistakes' the better. Soon she was just tossing stuff on with the rest of us."

Erica, who had built the giant plant puppets for the Los Angeles production of *Little Shop of Horrors*, designed the *Legend* set to fulfill writer Doug Haverty's request for a talking mountain – called Abra in the script. Abra had eyes that were operated from behind, a recirculating waterfall, and the temperamental fog machine. She was covered with vine and flower puppets; she even signed her lines through a craggy outcropping that was actually an interpreter in a rock costume. Her mouth opened up to spit out the hero Derek or swallow up the evil Mortigrim, all thanks to the busy technicians operating the set.

"We had a very active role and that was very exciting to me," remembers Tal Sanders, who worked on the *Legend* crew. "We weren't just pushing scenery, we were characters, puppeteers I guess you'd say, and we were giving life and character to this mountain. The vines and flowers grew and withered, the eyes and mouth moved; we had to run the waterfall. Many times the hearing crew would have to cue deaf actors from the mountain – maybe we would lift a flower at a certain point or move the eyes. It was very complicated, the timing was very tight, and we were often running around covering for little disasters that the audience never saw.

"I remember one performance where nothing had gone right for me," Tal continues. "At the end of the show, the crew got a curtain call – the cast would turn and gesture to the mountain and we were supposed to scurry up the ladders with the flower puppets on our hands and wave the flowers. So I scurried up the ladder and the ladder tipped over, and I fell behind the mountain. The audience didn't know the difference, it was just like a flower popped up and then it was gone. But Rod knew and he came running backstage saying 'I saw you come up, where'd you go, where'd you go?' And I'm lying stretched out groaning with this flower attached to my hand."

Legend's set was by far the most ambitious Access Theatre had ever attempted. It was enhanced with Pat Frank's fanciful lighting; Rod's sculpted, glowing, battery-operated crystals; and Pamela Shaw's costumes, including

Flavia Weedn's fears about seeing her paintings adapted to set designs were alleviated as soon as she met scenic designer Alison Yerxa. "When I said I thought the truck *(right)* should be the color of Campbell's tomato soup and she knew exactly what I meant, I knew things were going to work out," Flavia says. Engineer Gerald Brady of Lightweight Structural Designs built the *Flavia* set from balsa, foam, and muslin. All of it — even the big tree *(left)* and the house — broke down into tiny, light pieces that were easily packed and re-assembled like a jigsaw puzzle. *Flavia and the Dream Maker*, Center Stage Theater, 1991.

an ingenious mermaid-on-dry-land costume that was carefully integrated with actress Tamara Turner's wheelchair.

"That show fulfilled a fantasy for me of doing a show full of special effects and magic," Rod remembers. "I was up to my elbows in it and it was a blast. The technology wasn't that high tech, in fact it was pretty low tech, it just worked well. I remember standing in the back of the theater watching, and when someone would disappear into the waterfall or the crystals would glow in someone's hands you'd hear the kids in the audience go 'wow.' And I was thinking the same thing myself."

For years after *Legend* closed, the set was a mountain without a home. It was moved several times from garage to attic, finally coming to rest in Rod's parents' backyard. "It was like a dead body we were trying not to bury," Rod remembers wryly. "Finally," Reg Lathim says, "the time came. The garbage men were coming up the hill and we said 'this is the day.' We were literally out there in the street pushing it into the back of the garbage truck, crying, because so much work had gone into it. But I guess that's just part of theater."

Access Theatre began touring shows in 1981, when the sign language revue *Signing Off* went to county schools and other venues in California. Nearly every one of the subsequent shows toured as well. Along the way, the company adapted to virtually every kind of performing situation, from elementary school cafeterias to the Kennedy Center – and everything in between.

Rod and his designers learned to create sets, props, and costumes that packed and traveled easily. The company invested in modest, portable sound and projection equipment. They bought two vans, and rented countless others on the road. But there were some problems no amount of preparation could prevent.

"It was the lighting that killed us," remembers Tal Sanders. "Rod, John Kelly, and I would walk into a space and find out what they had. And sometimes it was a cakewalk and they had everything you could want – just point and throw the color and go. But I also remember a time when John and I spent about eight hours actually repairing lighting equipment so the lights would work. It was about 110 degrees in the ceiling of this theater in the middle of the summer in Palm Springs. And John and I are up there sweating buckets trying to get enough light together to do the show.

"We never knew in the morning when we moved in to a theater what the rest of the day was going to be like," Tal continues. "Actually it was exciting. And it's really not that different than most touring theaters. I mean you can send the lighting cues ahead and it may be in their contract to preprogram into the board. But 20 or 30 percent of the time you get there and they haven't done it. They say 'oh you wanted us to do it *before* you got here,' or 'yeah well, we just struck a show last night.'

"The same was true with accessibility," Tal concludes. "It didn't matter how much advance you did, you would still end up carrying Tami's wheelchair up and down steps, sometimes with her in it. It was just part of the job. Rod tends to use technicians that will fit into that style of working, who are willing to take on the responsibility, not as problems but as part of the job."

"You can't be the kind of person who looks at a broom and says, 'that's not my job, I don't sweep up, I'm the designer,'" Ted adds. "If it needs sweeping, you sweep."

Between 1988 and 1996, during the six

years that *Storm Reading* toured, Access Theatre came of age technically. While *Storm Reading* was touring, the company mounted three full Equity shows back in Santa Barbara, and the influence of Equity stage manager Kathleen Parsons helped formalize the technical policies for all the shows.

Storm Reading toured to more than 150 venues throughout the United States and abroad. The design incorporated simple sculptural set pieces and projected slides – elements that could be adapted to almost any venue – and went through numerous transformations, each one a little easier to pack and transport. Rod and company manager Thom Rollerson learned the art of advancing a tour, and the crew learned to overcome obstacles – from equipment failure to accessibility problems to the wholly unexpected.

"We arrived in Scottsdale and the stage had levels with about a six-inch step up between them," remembers technical director John Kelly, who traveled with the show for three years. "I don't care who you are, no one's that good in a wheelchair.

"We had a rider that went with the contract that was supposed to insure accessibility," John continues. "We tried to call ahead and ask the basic questions: Is there a dressing room for our star that's on stage level, and if not is there an elevator? If not where can he dress? There were at least a couple of times when we had to set up a bivouac area in the wings for Neil's dressing room because there was nothing accessible."

Storm Reading was mounted successfully for bookings that ranged from a banquet hall with no stage lights at all, to the infamous Ford's Theatre in Washington D.C. In the days before the ADA, however, fame did not guarantee accessibility. "Ford's doesn't have wheelchair seating down front," John says. "We tried to get some ramping in the aisles, but never got anywhere. It was a union house and also a National Parks Service building, so there were lots of regulations. You can't do anything to the building without checking in with the Park Service. They'd say 'well we have five or six wheelchair seats.' We'd say 'what if forty people show up in wheelchairs?' The show had a pretty big reputation and we knew people would come, and they did, and they didn't have anywhere to sit.

"We had to be on it all the time. So much of this stuff was so new to people, it was as if we were the pioneers arriving in an uncharted land."

Two words: traffic patterns.

"It was a way of life," Rod says, referring to the logistical dance required to accommodate wheelchairs and other accessibility elements. "In fact traffic patterns were a classic part of all our shows. It's not something the audience notices, but boy did we have them. In *Stage Struck* it was like pedestrians on a bike path where half the people were rolling and half the people were walking. As part of the rehearsal process, everyone learned this extended choreography both on stage and behind the scenes. They had to learn how to be in an environment where people were walking, rolling, hearing, not hearing, seeing, not seeing. We always used to say that a power wheelchair only rolled over someone's toes once.

"Backstage we had to have things planned," Rod continues. "There were times when people needed to be there to hold back curtains so somebody could zoom on or off, or scenery could come on or off. Someone using a wheelchair might have to enter first and the scenery come on after him, or the scenery might have to go off first so the person in the wheelchair wouldn't end up blocked backstage.

Ted Dolas' design for *At Long Last Leo*, brought a real middle American backyard to the intimate Center Stage Theater. "Wonderfully detailed," wrote *Drama-Logue* critic Susan Stewart Potter. "The set, complete with real grass which Dad mows, even has the bedroom and service porch visible through the windows. Infiltrated with all the accoutrements of the mundane (fertilizer, rags, mops, weeds) the set, (like another character) provides the constant note of the thing Leo is fighting against."

"The audience was sitting just a few feet away," Ted says, "Somehow I felt having the warmth of real grass in front of them was important. It's tactile, it's even got a smell. They're watching this lost soul and this dysfunctional family so I thought the grass would be grounding, something real to grab onto."

At Long Last Leo
Center Stage Theater, 1991.

The 1984 production, *Kites*, vividly created an afternoon in the park with no set other than colorful kites, which flew over the stage and out into the audience under the supervision of stage manager David Johnson, who also made sure the wind blew, the actors flew, the rain fell, and the neon rainbow appeared. L.K. Strasburg's lighting, and props including giant picnic foods, completed the imaginative stage pictures. *Kites*, Lobero Theatre, 1984.

Because Access Theatre's summer musical *Leap!* did not tour, designer Tal Sanders didn't worry about the set's weight or portability, and went for dramatic visual pictures. *Leap!* featured two very different sets: a high tech modern structure featuring scaffolding, platforms, and video projection *(above)*, and an earthy sculptural set in greens and browns *(below left)*. The show incorporated double harness flying, and more than 300 lighting, slide, video, and sound cues. *(Above left)* actor Judson Morgan argues with his teacher Tony Miratti, who appears only on video. Sets and technical design were executed entirely by student crew under the supervision of Sanders and stage manager Peter McCorkle.

Leap! Santa Barbara High School Center for the Performing Arts, 1995.

There were visual cues for deaf actors, and audio cues for blind actors – sometimes hundreds of cues within a production – all mapped out."

When the company moved into a theater, the crew had a checklist that included taping cables down securely so people using wheelchairs could roll over them. Props would be positioned exactly so an actor who was blind could find them in an instant. People were teamed up for costume changes, and many shared microphones. "Backstage you were still in the show, every second," Rod says. "No one could let down, because they all had responsibilities."

Building accessibility elements into a show was not simply a matter of logistics, it was part of the company's artistic philosophy. "It reflected that spirit of inclusion," says sign language interpreter Michael Purcell. Accessibility takes a lot more work and a lot more time, and sometimes you say to yourself 'why can't we just do a regular show?' But when you finally achieve access, where you get an element to work and satisfy all of the people concerned, you realize it was the best choice anyway. You realize the accessible choice was the most creative, original, artistic choice you could have made."

Accessibility was not only a backstage issue, but extended into the audience as well. Long before the ADA was a gleam in a legislator's eye, good wheelchair seating and sign language interpretation were available at every Access performance. Volunteer Joan Levy brailled Access Theatre's programs for years. In 1991, the company acquired an assistive listening system – the Phonic Ear Easy Listener – which amplifies music, sound effects, and the actors' voices in a headset via an FM receiver. It was used by the company to broadcast translations to Spanish-speaking audience members as well.

The Phonic Ear system was also the technical foundation for the company's audio description program, started in 1991 by the company's Accessibility Services Director Sue Dumm. "Audio description is the art of describing visual information for audience members who are blind or partially sighted. The describer relates actions, body language, lights, costumes, scenery, or other aspects of the performances that are not conveyed by the performers' voices." Sue says. "You use your voice much like an actor might use his hands, but there is a fine line between making it interesting and giving an opinion about the action."

In 1995, through the leadership of Dr. Joseph Pollock, Access Theatre acquired the Infosign open captioning system by Rapidtext, Inc. With this system, used for *Leap!*, *Storm Reading*, and the company's Young Playwrights Festivals, scripts are typed into a portable laptop computer and appear as scrolling text during the performance. For the company's benefit premiere of Michael Douglas' film *Disclosure*, the system was operated by a stenographer to provide real-time captioning for the speakers and the film.

The audience accessibility programs, supported by donations and volunteers, were among the company's most successful legacies. Access Theatre didn't just incorporate these services into its own performances, but lobbied hard to get stage and movie theaters throughout Santa Barbara and Los Angeles to use the services. The company toured with all audience accessibility services – the only national touring company to do so. Company manager Thom Rollerson and program director Daniel Girard spent hours in advance of an engagement getting the word out to audiences. "We would go into cities large and small, introduce these services and create audience interest," Thom says, "When we left, people were empowered to speak up and keep it going. We left a trail of awareness with audience members all over the country about what they could get in the theater."

Altogether, Rod and company gave hundreds of hours of workshops and consultations to help implement accessibility across the United States and as far away as Japan. In 1992, Access Theatre became headquarters for the Association for Theatre and Accessibility, and Rod served as president of the organization until 1996. During those years, Access Theatre was the flagship of the ATA – the model of what professional theater could achieve in creating accessibility for both audience and artists.

— ·— —

When Access Theatre launched Youth Access to the Arts, the company wanted to give students a complete, real-world experience of theater, including technical and accessibility aspects. The students, mostly junior high and high school age, built the set and ran the tech for the company's youth productions of *Godspell* and *Leap!*. They also produced the company's music videos "It's in Every One of Us" and "Focus."

"We really wanted them to learn how to do a show right – how to build things correctly, how to draft and weld, how cues are written, how to call them efficiently and effectively, how to run spotlights – all the technical jobs and why they are important," says Tal Sanders, designer for both of the Youth Access stage productions.

"I felt like we did our job if we could make them understand that close is not close enough," Tal says. "Mistakes pile up – three inches off here and three inches off there, and pretty soon it doesn't look anything like what we wanted it to look like. When every little thing is right the whole picture can soar. I think we were a little tougher on them than they were used to. Growth potential is not realized if you let them get away with things, and in the end they responded really well."

"When you worked on an Access Theatre show, you couldn't expect a routine," Ted concludes. "You didn't have a huge staff running around – there wasn't one guy who came in just to put up the molding. As a designer you didn't get to go off in a corner, draw the picture, and hand it off to be built. You *did* get a chance to explore. You were a collaborator in a serious design process. I would imagine that students and designers who are serious about doing really creative design would gravitate to a theater like Access. You can't expect to win a Tony, you won't be paid for overtime, and you don't get to work with all the big fancy toys. But at the same time, you're not going to pick up your contract and realize you're doing the millionth production of *Guys and Dolls* and that's it. You will never just be grinding out the fourth show of the season and punching the clock."

Jonathan Sabo's original set for *Storm Reading*
on stage at Ford's Theatre, Washington D.C.

accessibility checklist

for audiences

> Physical access to theater for people using mobility aids including wheelchairs, walkers or canes: this includes ADA specified elements including ramps; accessible bathrooms, drinking fountains, and box office window; a variety of accessible, level seating for people using wheelchairs, with seating for companions; and elevators or lifts to other than ground floor levels

> Text telephone in the box office and on the theater information line; trained box office staff to use text telephone and regional relay phone service for deaf patrons

> Sign language interpreters (preferably onstage and shadowing the actors) using translations that have been evaluated by local deaf consultants

> Open captioning for deaf or hard of hearing people who do not understand sign language. A second language translation may be offered via this system if appropriate.

> Assistive listening headphones (infrared or FM) to magnify sound for people who are hard of hearing. A second language translation may be offered via this system if appropriate.

> Cassettes and portable cassette systems with pre-recorded information on the theater, layout, programming, sponsors, etc. for patrons who are blind or partially sighted

> Brailled literature and programs

> Audio description service (infrared or FM system) for patrons who are blind or partially sighted with audio descriptions evaluated by local blind consultants.

> Pre-performance tactile tours of sets and costumes for audience members who are blind or partially sighted

> Ushers and house staff trained to demonstrate and explain access services

> Standardized logos to indicate accessibility services; prominent and consistent display of these logos on all theater promotion and advertising materials; specific promotion of accessibility services via the media and public information lines

accessibility checklist

for artists and technicians

> Physical access to stage, dressing rooms, bathrooms, technical control areas, orchestra pit and booth for artists using mobility aids including wheelchairs, walkers or canes

> Flashing light cueing system in green room and/or dressing rooms to cue deaf actors

> Audio monitors in green room and/or dressing room to cue blind artists

> Sign language interpreters for rehearsals/performances for deaf artists

> Brailled or recorded scripts

> Transportation to and from rehearsals and performances for artists who do not have vehicles equipped for their needs, or who are not able to use public transportation, either because of lack of accessibility or schedule limitations

> When touring, accessible transportation and accommodations for artists using mobility aids including wheelchairs, walkers or canes

Remi Sandri and Bobbie Beth Scoggins

Children of a Lesser God, Garvin Theatre, 1985

"The play is full of very human struggle and conflict," Rod says. "It gave hearing audiences their first taste of multidimensional deaf characters — people who were deaf and also stubborn and pig-headed and complex. A lot of people think that if you're disabled you're to be pitied and you're an angel who's overcoming so much. This play was honest about the fact that it didn't matter if you were deaf, you could still be an angel or a jerk. Or both. People needed to know that just because someone has a disability doesn't mean they're toting a halo."

three plays

The history of Access Theatre revolves primarily around original works – fifteen original musicals and plays produced between 1979 and 1995. However, during that time, the company also mounted acclaimed productions of established plays and hosted one-man and one-woman creations by artists with disabilities.

These productions gave the company a break from the enormous responsibility of making new work. They allowed Rod to explore his skills as a director and actor, and they brought in Equity guest artists, some with disabilities, to collaborate with veteran Access Theatre performers.

In this way, the company got a sense of being connected to the larger world of theater. At the same time, the world of theater got a chance to see what non-traditional casting could bring to productions. Access Theatre proved that the existing body of theatrical literature could be more accessible to actors and audiences while maintaining, and even enhancing, the original intent of the plays.

———

Mark Medoff's *Children of a Lesser God* won the 1980 Tony Awards for its two leads, including the first such award for a deaf actress, Phyllis Frelich as the headstrong Sarah. That same year, Rod was working on his second production, *Through Our Eyes*. He knew nothing of the groundbreaking play that was dazzling audiences on Broadway. When Michael Douglas told him about "the new play with a deaf lead," Rod could hardly imagine that five years later he would be invited to direct *Children* himself. He was "delighted and frankly terrified" when the Santa Barbara Repertory Theatre proposed a co-production, with Rod as director.

For the first time in his directing career, other people were there to worry about the set and the publicity. Rod threw himself into casting the play, auditioning deaf actresses all over the country for his Sarah before deciding on a vibrant Equity actress, Bobbie Beth Scoggins. Ian Edward Kelly, veteran of several national and international productions, would reprise his role of Orin.

Alongside the professionals, Rod cast a first-time, hard-of-hearing actress Marnee Wafer in a supporting part and gambled on 24-year-old Remi Sandri in the pivotal role of James Leeds.

Remi was just three years into his acting career, and had recently moved from Santa Barbara to New York to study. He had already appeared in productions throughout Southern California, including Access Theatre's *Stage Struck*. Even so, the role was a stretch for any young actor. James Leeds was on stage for virtually the entire play, and the portrayal could make or break the production.

Rod flew to New York and auditioned Remi for three days – at the Circle in the Square Theatre where he was studying, in the park, and at his apartment building. Together they tried nearly every scene in the play before Rod was sure.

At the library at Lincoln Center, Rod watched the original Broadway production on videotape and took "copious notes," looking for anything to help him face the intimidating prospect of directing his first established play. Back home, when rehearsals began, Rod literally threw the notes away when his two leads dug into their characters with what he remembers as "a kind of fearlessness and a willingness to try anything." Rod was now confident he could create an original interpretation, and found the give and take with his actors a rewarding challenge.

Yet even with rehearsals going so well, the truth remained that Remi was faced with a daunting task, to learn and perform a big, emotional role in two languages simultaneously – English and American Sign Language. "It was *the* hardest thing I've ever had to do," Remi remembers. "The syntax for the English words and the sign aren't always the same, so it's not so straightforward as one sign per word. ASL is very much its own language. Peter Robertson my coach was a perfectionist about that, and an amazing taskmaster – 'no, higher up on the body, no keep it inside this zone, no make this bigger for the stage, you're hands aren't sharp enough here, it's *this* shape, not this shape,' just drilling me and drilling

Remi Sandri, Marnee Wafer, Francine Buker
Children of a Lesser God, Garvin Theatre, 1985

First-time actress Marnee Wafer played Lydia, a hard-of-hearing character who speaks. "She just nailed it," Rod recalls, "just walked away with the scene. My process with her was completely different than with the rest of the cast. I just encouraged her to be herself. That was enough."

"Too funny for words," wrote the *Los Angeles Sentinel* of comedian Charles (C.J.) Jones' one-man show, *The Living Cartoon*. "Hilarious" and "brilliant," wrote others. "The coolest," pronounced another, who noted the "...almost constant, spontaneous laughter from the young audience."

In his energetic show, C.J. is, among many things, a one-man baseball game, a cowboy, and an ill-fated gorilla in love. He involves the audience, calling for volunteers to become a roller coaster or a washing machine, and they rush to comply.

C.J. comes from a family of eight children, all hearing, born to deaf parents. He became deaf at age seven, the result of spinal meningitis, and admits to being a comedian since "I left my mama's womb." An internationally known entertainer, he received a special Tony Award in 1977 for his work with the National Theater of the Deaf, and appeared in the national touring production of *Children of a Lesser God.* He was a regular on *Sesame Street* and the PBS show *Rainbow's End* and has appeared on NBC's *A Different World.*

In 1993, Access Theatre began presenting C.J.'s *The Living Cartoon* in schools, conferences, and theaters throughout the United States, with a special focus on young audiences. C.J.'s effect on kids has been stunning. They are completely won over into his fast-paced world of visual gags, and underlying lessons about deafness. "Swarmed like a rock star by tiny autograph hounds," observed one reporter of the post-performance pandemonium.

"You're the only person that can make me laugh more than TV," writes a high school student who is hard-of-hearing. From an admiring fifth grader: "You taught me that with a little encouragement you can do anything." Writes another student: "My friends have more respect for me after watching your performance and seeing a successful hard-of-hearing person." "That," C.J. says, "is the power of laughter. They see me as a human being. It teaches kids to appreciate who they are and to see others as a whole person."

me, until I could start to trust my hands to tell the story. Then, just when I'd start to get it right, I would hit the emotional scenes in the play and I'd want to go back to what is native to me, which is the spoken word. So my signs would just kind of crumple up on each other.

"Sometimes I went home from rehearsal and cried from frustration because it was like learning to communicate all over again. In that context I was definitely the person with the disability.

"It wasn't just about learning the signs," Remi adds, "it was learning a language. Of course I went through all the typical hearing things, 'oh, it's such a *beautiful* language, it's so *expressive*.' And it is all that, but deaf people look at you like 'uh huh.' It's sort of like someone coming up to me and saying, 'English is such a *great* language, oh God, can I just hear you talk?'"

At a local coffee shop after rehearsal, while the cast of deaf actors and interpreters signed among themselves, Remi practiced eagerly. "I'd start to think, 'OK, I'm getting this,' and then I'd look down to take a bite of my sandwich." When he looked back up, the conversation had flowed on without him.

"I remember Ed (Ian Kelly) would test

me. He'd come up and sign a bunch of stuff at me and I'd just nod and smile. And he'd go 'what'd I say?' I'd go 'I have no idea.' And he'd say 'That's right, and if you don't know, ask me.' So then he'd come up and sign at me again and look at me intently, like he wanted a response. And I'd say 'you signed nothing to me, that was gibberish, what do you want?' and he'd say 'OK Good. Good.'"

After four weeks of intense rehearsal, *Children of A Lesser God* opened to rave reviews. Remi received a local theater award for best performance of the year, a performance he believes was shaped in large part by sign language.

"I had come to theater with what I thought were really high standards, but what was actually a kind of rigidity, and a pushiness," Remi recalls. "I tended to make very fast choices in rehearsal and push others at that pace – to make it better, I thought. But that play really taught me to slow down as an actor. I was working in a second language so I couldn't rush my choices. I had to take the journey *with* other people, instead of hurrying ahead to the goal and looking back like, 'well, are you coming?'

"Rod made rehearsal a very safe place

Ian Edward Kelly and Remi Sandri

Children of a Lesser God, Garvin Theatre, 1985

"When I first started playing Orin [in the Milwaukee company] I was twenty-three and I played him very angry," Ed says. "Over the years, my portrayal changed. As I grew older and understood more about deaf rights and the politics of what deaf people are fighting for, Orin became more of an activist and less of a rebel. I watched and learned from people who were active in the deaf community. In the end, I saw him as a powerful person, not an *angry* person."

Ed, who was born hard-of-hearing into a totally deaf family, played Orin for four years, in six national and international companies as well as in Access Theatre's production. He performed with several Los Angeles theater companies, appeared on the series *Beauty and the Beast*, and consulted on the Gene Wilder/ Richard Pryor comedy *See No Evil, Hear No Evil*, which generated controversy for casting a hearing actor in a deaf role.

Even with his professional credits, opportunities were scarce and Ed, who speaks, was frustrated to be typecast as deaf. He went on to work as an advocate with the Greater Los Angeles Council on Deafness, and as an audience development consultant for the Mark Taper Forum in Los Angeles.

"I understand the discrimination deaf people face, but I also understand from my work that people need to be individuals. Sometimes you get it from both sides, because the deaf community *wants* you to be deaf, and the hearing community discriminates against you *because* you are deaf. So either way I'm deaf before I'm an actor, I'm deaf before I'm a man. I know how limiting that feels. So I was incorporating all that experience into my portrayal of Orin and of course my life."

for us to explore together. You have to have a lot of confidence to walk out on stage and say 'Here, I have something.' You have to believe some part of you is worthy. Rod brings that out of you in a very interactive way. It was just a spirit of 'you can do anything,' That went for all of us in that company, not just people with disabilities – all our little failings could be absorbed and transformed."

———

Halfway through *The Boys Next Door*, Norman Bulansky goes to a dance. An appealing man with a developmental disability, a job at Eller's Donuts, and a fondness for the merchandise, he is eager to woo his Sheila, the quintessential girl behind the glasses. Their courtship is sweet, humorous, and a little surreal. As they grip onto each other and shuffle together to "Flashdance," they gradually become more graceful until, if you squint hard, they bear just the slightest resemblance to Fred Astaire and Ginger Rogers.

This scene, among others, earned freshman actress Susan Kern a prestigious *Drama-Logue* award for her portrayal of Sheila in Access Theatre's 1990 production of Tom Griffin's *The Boys Next Door*.

Kern is living with a head injury that affects her speech, motor responses and emotions. She had virtually no acting experience, but in Rod's words "she simply *was* the character." She was also one of the most determined personalities to ever pass through Access Theatre, and would come all the way from Florida to get her big break.

The Boys Next Door tells the story of four men with developmental disabilities who share an apartment under the long-suffering supervision of their social worker. The men range in function from severely retarded to merely compulsive. The play is both gut-wrenching and hilarious, as the five men struggle to get along and face their personal traumas and triumphs.

Though *Boys* was not a new work, it was a very high pressure production for Access Theatre. Opening in August of 1990, it was to be the inaugural performance for Santa Barbara's new Center Stage Theater. A backstage superstition says the success of the first production predicts the success of the theater; but more mundane concerns also loomed – would the brand new space be painted and rigged in time for the $100-a-seat opening night benefit?

"The first time I saw her and heard her speak I thought 'she *is* Sheila,'" Rod remembers of first-time actress and *Drama-Logue* award winner Susan Kern. "All she had to do was *like* Norman (Dirk Blocker) and she did. All she had to do was stay honest. And Dirk, who is such a gifted actor, was so giving and patient. They played off each other beautifully. They made each other laugh. And she lit up like a torch when she heard the audience laugh. She learned what incredible food laughter is."

Susan Kern and Dirk Blocker

The Boys Next Door, Center Stage Theater, 1990

Further, Rod had chosen *Boys* against the advice of board members who worried that the story would be patronizing, depressing, and funny for the wrong reasons. Remembering his own experiences with actors with developmental disabilities ten years earlier, Rod was less concerned. He saw humor, humanity, and deep affection in Griffin's characters; given the right actors he knew he could bring those qualities out.

The auditions drew a huge turnout, some three hundred hopefuls for eleven roles. Rod cast film actor Anthony Edwards (now star of NBC's *ER*) and a group of first-class Equity performers with a long list of credits in stage, film, and television. Rod was not specifically looking for a completely inexperienced actress to round out his cast. But Susan was absolutely determined to get the role.

Susan Kern was a sophomore nursing student in Miami when her car was hit head on by a drunk driver. The accident was nearly fatal – she suffered fourteen broken bones and a severe head injury. When she woke up from a three-month coma, she began years of frustrating physical therapy, at first in a wheelchair. Eventually she learned to walk, speak, and drive again.

Susan could not return to nursing, but another career had caught her imagination. She was going to be an actress, she was quite sure about that. Friends reminded her that it's tough for any actor to make it, much less an actress with a disability. One friend recalled her reaction to the advice: "She registered it, contemplated it for a second, and then just blew it off."

Susan began calling agents all over Miami, but her slowed speech pattern was immediately an obstacle. Most people assumed she had a developmental disability, and she was swiftly dismissed. When Access Theatre came to Miami's Coconut Grove Playhouse, Susan was in the audience. Minutes after the curtain call she cornered company manager Thom Rollerson. A month later, she flew to Los Angeles for Access Theatre's *Boys Next Door* auditions at the Mark Taper Forum.

Some 100 actresses, including well-known Hollywood veterans, auditioned for the part of Sheila. It went to Susan for what Rod saw as "a certain presence, personality, and glow. She had this really incredible, infectious laugh," Rod recalls, "and when she really got going you were laughing right along with her."

Richard Hochberg and Anthony Edwards

The Boys Next Door, Center Stage Theater, 1990

"Hockberg's portrayal is packed with nuance," wrote the *Los Angeles Times*. "Charged with lightning," added the *Santa Barbara News-Press*. "Edwards shows us a deeply caring man...but outstanding as it is, [his] performance is but one part of a seamless ensemble piece," wrote the *Santa Barbara Independent*.

Company, *The Boys Next Door*, Center Stage Theater, 1990. "The beauty of this production is that one comes away feeling that good actors have given their all," raved the *Los Angeles Times*.

On a Sunday morning in September of 1989, on his way home from a tennis match, film and TV veteran Art Metrano stopped to check up on a house he was selling. He climbed a ladder for some last minute tidying up, and moments later fell twelve feet squarely onto his head. Laying on the dirt and gravel in the Beverly Hills sunshine, unable to speak or move and struggling to breathe, he began to write the jokes that would become his one-man show *Twice Blessed*.

Although his first, second, and seventh vertebrae were broken, Metrano recovered to the point where he could walk with one crutch. In the process of repairing his body, the fifty-something, Brooklyn-raised comedian evaluated the whole of his troubled life from a new vantage point.

The result of his soul-searching premiered at the Hollywood Playhouse in 1992 and was remounted by Access Theatre the following year, adding interpreter Jo Black *(above with Metrano)*. Written with award-winning playwright Cynthia Lee, *Twice Blessed* is an intimate, free-ranging, and uncensored confessional spiced with dark humor. Metrano, best known for his portrayal of the frenzied Lt. Mauser in the *Police Academy* films, serves up jokes in the face of his adversity, which included an abused childhood, a point-blank shooting in a New York parking garage, and ultimately his accident and recovery. Two hours with Metrano (and without intermission), the show was called by critics "irresistibly shocking" and "gripping and triumphant."

Metrano's career began when "The Amazing Metrano" comedy/magic act premiered on the Johnny Carson show. His television roles have spanned the decades from *Hotel* and *Fantasy Island* to *Hill Street Blues* and *LA Law* — and since his accident, *Nurses* and *Silk Stalkings*. "I was blessed with adversity," Metrano told the *Los Angeles Times*. "I've learned to accept the limitations of my body. I know now it doesn't define who I am, or what I can yet become."

Marc Buckland and Henry Holden

The Boys Next Door, Center Stage Theater, 1990

Haven Mitchell, Marc Buckland, Dirk Blocker
and Richard Hochberg are The Boys Next
Door; Anthony Edwards *(center)*, is their
beleaguered shepherd.

"Buckland dominates a whole scene without speaking or moving," *the Los Angeles Times* wrote of his portrayal of the schizophrenic, golf-obsessed Barry, crushed by a devastating reunion with his abusive father. "...he simply exudes more and more intensity until the scene explodes emotionally."

165

The Boys Next Door was a delight. The ensemble shone, with outstanding portrayals from the leads and from supporting players, including Kellie Diamond, who has a developmental disability; veteran TV and stage actor Henry Holden; and deaf actress Billie Burke Perkins. Any initial fears about the material were allayed when the play turned out to be very funny, and for the right reasons.

"There are healthy laughs and gentle tears," wrote critic Richard Scaffidi in *Drama-Logue*. "There are characters to love and ideas to prize. Mostly, there is the steady, stirring beat of this show's huge heart."

Los Angeles *Drama-Logue* awards went to the production as a whole, to Rod for direction, and to Susan for performance. Her portrayal of Sheila was pronounced "astonishing" and "profoundly memorable" by critics. For her it was a very personal accomplishment.

"For years I felt so inferior to everyone because of the way I walked and talked," Susan says. "Now I'm starting to get some confidence back. I know that I'm always going to be disabled, but I'm tryin' my hardest to make it cool."

In the summer of 1990, Rod sat in the audience at the Ashland Shakespeare Festival watching Mark Stein's play *At Long Last Leo*. In the visionary but misguided Leo, he saw a character he wanted to play, and a story with the poignant bite of a modern-day *Don Quixote*. *At Long Last Leo* went into rehearsal at Access Theatre in April of 1991 with Rod in the lead role.

Rod had appeared in productions off and on throughout Access Theatre's history, but it had been five years since he had been on the stage. He had never attempted such a large or risky role as an actor. The odds went up when Emmy-award winning actress Bonnie Bartlett, then star of the hit series *St. Elsewhere*, turned down a movie-of-the week and joined the cast as Leo's mother. His fiery, flaky sister would be played by Victoria Ann Lewis, a respected stage actress, polio survivor, and regular on the nighttime soap *Knott's Landing*. Rod's portrayal of the fanatical, tragicomic Leo would have to be first rate.

At Long Last Leo is the story of a compulsive do-gooder who returns home armed with a 638-page "Manifesto." His save-the-

(left to right) Chet Carlin, Rod Lathim and Bonnie Bartlett

At Long Last Leo, Center Stage Theater, 1991

"Lathim effectively balances Leo's lighter and darker natures with infectious enthusiasm and anti-social resignation: he's a kind of prophet riding an emotional roller coaster," wrote *Daily Variety* critic Mike Frym. "This Mohammed meets his mountain in the persona of Bartlett, whose desperate angst produces almost tangible pathos." Bartlett's performance was unanimously praised for its "unsettling precision" and "a kind of stage presence that keeps the audience's eyes riveted."

world plan applies the Theory of Relativity to averting a "global thermonuclear anxiety attack." So sure is Leo of his revelations that his frustration is boundless when the world, and worst of all his family, cannot see what is so obvious, so brilliant, so essential to the future of mankind.

Though it does not deal specifically with issues of physical disability, the play begs the question "what is disability?" in a spectacularly dysfunctional family. Stein's script presents a smorgasbord of maladies from the clinical depression of Leo's mother and the unfocused philandering of his father, to the hardbitten defenses of his sister. For the Access Theatre production, award-winning Los Angeles director Frank Condon crafted a realistic comedic drama that would be called "masterful," "stunning" and "impeccable," by critics. On a backyard set with real grass, the characters merged in a realistic portrait of middle-class angst, with Leo as the strident, unsung prophet at the center. "A funny-sad, and ultimately uplifting production," praised the *Los Angeles Times*.

Even so, the rehearsal process for *At Long Last Leo* was one of Rod's most painful experiences in the theater. His naturally posi-

tive persona and background in musical comedy, left him unprepared for the darker sides of a role that hit very close to home.

Though Rod's visions had come true in the success of Access Theatre, Leo faced indifference to his message, most painfully from his own family. This touched some deep emotions for Rod. "I related to this character in a very personal way," he recalls now. "And I needed to go places with the character I didn't want to go."

Rod, who also had a full-time job as the play's producer – found the process of developing Leo's character draining and exasperating. He resisted making the commitment, as if he could somehow do the work with just a part of himself, as if he didn't have to reveal anything too personal. And it was a difficult role, especially given Rod's relative inexperience as a dramatic actor.

Veteran actress Bonnie Bartlett, who played Leo's skeptical, negative mother, had no patience for Rod's struggle. Soon life was imitating art, as the two leads clashed in rehearsals. "Bonnie's attitude was like a hard, swift kick in the ass," Rod says, "and it left me with a choice – quit or dig in harder. I ended up using the frustration I felt with Bonnie and

In 1995, Access Theatre presented *Belle's on Wheels*, a loosely autobiographical one-woman show by actress/writer Jaehn Clare. In 1980, Jaehn fell 27 feet from a catwalk access ladder in the theater at the University of South Dakota and broke her back. After an 18-month absence, she finished her B.A. in theater at the University of Minnesota and went on to get her Masters at the University of Essex in Colchester, England. *Belle's on Wheels* was originally written as her dissertation and was performed throughout the U.K.

The semi-fictional episodes of Jaehn's play draw on her experiences with a life-changing spinal cord injury, the frustration of reentering the professional theatrical world, and the challenge of overcoming her fears and the fears of other people. The result — infused with Jaehn's perspective on love, relationships, and things female — is a modern journey through a life rocked by change, and what one local reviewer called "vibrant theater, dark humor and a quest for clarity."

The Access Theatre production was the first staging of the play with full technical support, including Ted Dolas' lighting and scenic design created specifically for the production. It was also the first time the play was presented with shadow sign language interpretation, by Michael Purcell. "We made an artistic choice to use the shadow interpreting method," Jaehn says, "so Michael was always very close to me. We also on occasion blurred the distinction between me as a performer and Michael as intepreter, as when he took on the presence of other characters in my monologues. It stands as my most satisfying and gratifying performance experience with that show, not just because of his skill as a signer, but his sensitivity and skill as a collaborator, as a performer."

the insecurity it brought out in me to go deeper into the character."

In the end, though the critics acknowledged the script's potential to "plunge into bathos," all praised the ensemble acting and Rod's hard-won performance. "Lathim gives us Leo excited and hopeful at one moment and nearly fascistic the next," wrote *Drama-Logue* critic Susan Stewart Potter. "It's an energetic and believable portrait of a desperate man utterly caught up in hope without the balance of reality." "Lathim's rapport with Leo as a fellow visionary was obviously the reason for selecting the play in the first place," observed Phillip Brandes in the *Los Angeles Times*, "His performance is absolutely convincing – we feel he's walked many miles in Leo's shoes."

"I wanted to be challenged by a character that had anger and temper," Rod says, "as opposed to what I've always been known as – the guy with the eternal smile. Leo was not a smiler. He was a thinker. It showed me that I have darkness in me, a side of me that can be very out there. It's not a side I promote or cultivate, but it's there. It shocked my family and close friends when they saw it come out on stage. It temporarily shattered my image as a nurturer and person who wants to please.

"We all need variety in our artistic lives," Rod concludes. "I always said I wanted to do a role that was as far from musical theater as you can get, and Leo was definitely that. It was an emotional journey for me every night. The battle on stage was very real for me, more real than I could have imagined when I chose that play for myself. I must say, I had no idea when I started down that road, what I was letting myself in for."

Bonnie Bartlett *(foreground)* with *(left to right)* Chet Carlin, Tyler Dumm and Victoria Ann Lewis, *At Long Last Leo*, Center Stage Theater, 1991

"She cuts right through the crap in just about every scene she's in," wrote the *Drama-Logue* critic of Santa Barbara actress Delta Giordano Morgan as Leo's down-to-earth neighbor and girlfriend. "Without guile and with perfect comic timing...her performance is rather like the pure sound of a flute rising above the cacophony of the unhappy family."

Rod Lathim and Delta Giordano Morgan
At Long Last Leo, Center Stage Theater, 1991

Clockwise from top: Michael Purcell, Noah Gaines,

Clarke Thorell and Anne Jacoby, "Fly,"

Flavia and the Dream Maker, Center Stage Theater, 1991

the dream makers

The first day of rehearsals poured with rain, as twelve-year-old Anne Jacoby settled quietly into her seat at Access Theatre's new building. Her co-stars were already gathered around the big table. One by one, Anne was introduced to some of the best friends she would make in her young life.

After months of auditions, Access Theatre had finally cast the company's new show, a musical based on the best-known of artist Flavia Weedn's illustrated stories. The script was nearly complete; composer Shelly Markham and lyricist Bob Garrett were putting the finishing touches on the witty '40s-inspired tunes. *Flavia and the Dream Maker* would open nine weeks later to enthusiastic audience response, with Anne in the leading role as 12-year-old Flavia and Clarke Thorell as her uncle and hero Jack.

Reviewers beamed over the sentimental little musical and the sincere performances of the cast; letters poured in from school children. *Flavia* was Access Theatre's largest financial investment to date and received a crush of publicity. Yet none of it was enough. The show never fulfilled its commercial potential or lived up to everyone's plans for it. Despite its considerable charms, *Flavia and the Dream Maker* ended too soon. But not before helping a talented but uncertain young girl grow up a little, get closer to her own dream, and learn something about herself from an extraordinary cast of characters.

———

The world of painter and author Flavia Weedn is wrapped in a soft romantic glow. Her greeting cards, books and hand-written aphorisms speak of simple truths and hope. Her heart-on-the sleeve optimism reaches millions of fans worldwide, who exchange her cards and gifts, collect them, and even pass them on to their children. Flavia's art is made to share and people do, with a passion.

Her autobiographical children's book, *Flavia and the Dream Maker*, was published in 1988. It is a simply told story of her awkward, Depression-era adolescence, made magical by her charismatic Uncle Jack – a WWII flyer who died when his B52 went down on its second-to-last mission. Jack left his young niece heartbroken, but inspired to pass on his transformative influence through her art. It was the kind of story Access Theatre knew how to tell. It also seemed ideal for the kind of commercially viable musical Rod wanted to do next.

The touring success of *Storm Reading* had convinced Rod that he should develop a show tailor-made to tour, with built-in international appeal. Rod and company had learned from *Storm Reading*. They knew what they needed for a successful tour – a set that was easy to pack, set up, and strike; contracts that guaranteed theater accessibility; and most of all, a show that was easy to sell in a few words. When Flavia's son Rick approached Rod with the idea for *Flavia and the Dream Maker*, he agreed.

Flavia lived in Santa Barbara and had been an Access Theatre fan for more than a

decade. "I knew I could not have sent it to someone, say, in New York, someone I didn't know or trust," she recalls. "I knew Access Theatre and I knew I could have a hand in it."

Playwright Doug Haverty, who had written *Legend of the Crystal Waters* for the company, was commissioned to write the new musical. He needed to expand Flavia's slim, evocative book – "something that was already perfect," he says – into a two-hour script. For the stage, he had to create dramatic conflict in a story that was mostly goodness and light; he needed to flesh out the sweet, watercolor characters. The only way to do it, he felt, was to get to know Flavia and – through her memories – her Uncle Jack.

"She painted such a picture of her life," Doug says of the process, which involved hours of interviews. "Her memories are frosty-clear; when she describes an emotion it is right there like you can touch it."

Flavia stuck close to the project, particularly in the early stages and was "very, very paternal" about it, she recalls. "Then a point came where the story and the background were clear enough to them that they could just go with it."

One night, Flavia invited the cast to her

"I remember my best compliment was from C.J. He said when I was singing, even though he couldn't hear everything, his heart was hearing me because he could just see it in my whole character and my expression. Then I knew my character was coming across and that made me feel so good."

Anne Jacoby
Flavia and the Dream Maker,
Center Stage Theater, 1991

home ("like a museum," Anne remembers). They stayed into the early hours of the morning listening to her stories. "There's a before and after for every character," Anne recalls, and she was fascinated by the details. She could also relate to Flavia's memories of feeling different and left out as a child, how Jack had given her confidence in herself, and how that confidence had helped her survive his loss.

After the others had gone, Anne stayed and spent the night surrounded by Flavia's tangible and intangible memories of Uncle Jack. "I didn't realize it yet," Anne says, "but I was going to learn from this show some of what Flavia had learned from Jack."

———

Clarke Thorell almost wasn't cast as Jack. At the final audition in Los Angeles, with his bright, frank singing voice he captured the vulnerable charm of a young man who leads without knowing it. But another actor had been cast, his voice a little more quintessentially Broadway, his style a little more sophisticated. A scheduling conflict arose and the part fell to Clarke – a twist of what Flavia would surely call Fate. "Clarke simply *was* Jack," she says and everyone agreed – except Clarke's

agent, who urged him not to take the part, even though the show was to be a professional, full Equity production.

"He didn't want me to be away from all the opportunity in L.A.," Clarke says, "But I was just starting out professionally and a lot of what was considered opportunity was not very fulfilling. I thought this was a chance to get some meaning out of my work."

The real-life Jack was young and optimistic, a ham, a charmer, a good son and a favorite uncle. He convinced Flavia to revel in being different; he could make dreams out of paper hats and everyday life. Though he had been dead for more than forty years, he was the driving force behind Flavia's story and the musical, and Clarke soon came under his spell.

"Jack was a person who savored life," he says. "One of the things I got from that experience was a sense of value in experiencing life fully moment to moment. It's not to say that I think every moment of a person's life or work is momentous. But for me, certain things became heightened through learning that sense of appreciation. Little things, like the ability to hear music. Food. Certain times of day, certain qualities of light. And not in that 'Oh my gosh look at that sunset' type of thing. It just

"Jack was one person telling a little girl that she can do anything. And look what happened," says Flavia.

Anne Jacoby and Clarke Thorell
Flavia and the Dream Maker, 1991

Deaf actress Fran Ripplinger
with Clarke Thorell

Flavia and the Dream Maker,
Center Stage Theater, 1991

seemed as if a feeling of appreciation became more readily available to me. And I learned to communicate about it and notice it in others.

"There are things that each of us responds to passionately, things that bring out the life in us. Everybody wants to be seen and appreciated for those things, and wants to share them with other people. Jack was about accessing that."

———·———

Fresh from playing the brash, cartoon-character lead in the musical *Annie*, Anne found the process of creating a real-life person in an original musical very difficult. She was in junior high in Santa Ynez, California, a bit of a misfit in the horsy, affluent school. Her passion for the arts mystified most of her classmates.

Every day Anne left school right at the final bell, starting her homework in the car as her mother drove the 45 minutes to rehearsal.

"It was difficult for the people at my school to understand what I was going through and to relate to the huge, astronomical dreams I had about what I wanted to become. I was going through the struggle of being different. I just had to find my own way.

But I felt like an alien.

"With *Flavia* I had to relate to an audience all these insecurities that I had never really exposed before. In the play, Flavia was terribly self-conscious and going through a hard time making friends and feeling comfortable with herself, and I was too. But Rod was always there helping me.

"I remember one time we took a walk by ourselves to a nearby park and we just talked. We were trying to break through into this character and we talked about how it's really hard when you're growing up, and how feeling accepted is a really difficult thing. He was so wonderful about making it totally personal. He didn't ignore the fact that I was going through things, and he really treated me as a person and not just as the character. I think that's a really great quality in a director at any time.

"Having that trust and faith in Rod really allowed me to break through, to do difficult things with the character and what she – and I – were going through.

"I wasn't always happy at school and I didn't always like how thirteen-year-olds treat each other; some people aren't always very nice. Going to rehearsal was sometimes such a relief because everyone was such a big family at Access. I realized at some point that they were very special people. They had all touched my life deeply.

"We were doing this show about an uncle helping his insecure niece. But a lot of it had to do with this wonderful cast helping Anne."

—·—

It was not all wonderful. New musicals are notoriously difficult. *Flavia* was a collaboration among well-established professionals, each with their own ambitions for the show, which seemed a sure winner, maybe even Broadway material. "Sometimes I felt more like a referee than a director," Rod says of the struggles to get the story, the songs, and the casting right, while maintaining the company's commitment to accessible theater.

The show was uniquely successful in that respect. Patty Neumeyer, who is partially sighted, was cast in a part that was not written to be blind. The narrator, played by deaf actor C.J. Jones, used both sign language and speech. Only Fran Ripplinger, who is deaf, played a character with a disability: Mammo, Flavia's grandmother, was written as deaf, and created a logical reason for the cast to sign.

Sign language interpreter Michael Purcell was written into the show as a character and naturally integrated into the action.

In the rehearsal process, the cast all learned to sign their parts and songs, even Patty, who had to learn sign language by feel. Co-star C.J. was her salvation "He had a joke to go with each sign," Patty remembers, "and we would make taped descriptions so I could go home and practice. It was funny, he had to really work at the musical numbers because he couldn't hear the music, which was the most natural part for me, and I had to really memorize and work at the signs."

In hours of sign language rehearsals, Michael paired the cast up and let them learn by doing – no talking allowed. "On stage it had to seem like we were saying things in sign for the first time," Clarke says, "so it wasn't enough to just learn the sign. We had to learn to really *listen* in sign so we could respond naturally.

"Fran and C.J. especially were always there to call me on my BS," Clarke continues. "If I was tuning out, if I wasn't completely there, completely listening, they didn't let me get away with it. It's funny how I learned to listen from them. They use their senses in a different way, but that idea of listening came through so clearly. I learned to listen through using sight, through awareness of myself and my environment. As an actor, that allows you to draw a more honest response. All that listening stayed with me."

When Clarke was 11 years old he had his first experience with sign language. He was hired to portray a deaf child for a poster for a major national charity. "The poster said 'after two years of therapy Ricky said thank you' and I was Ricky, signing 'thank you,'" Clarke recalls. "It's pretty shocking now, but at the time I was too young to understand."

After *Flavia* Clarke got a call to portray a deaf person in a national commercial. "I asked, 'will you be using deaf people?' They said they would like to, but they would rather have hearing people who knew how to sign. I objected, not in a confrontational way, I just pointed out that there are deaf people who are able to work and want to be working in this field. I wasn't called back.

"If it hadn't been for my experience with Access I'm not sure I would have spoken up about that, but now for me it's like people in blackface playing someone of African descent. Obviously Dustin Hoffman can play a person who is autistic. Good actors should be able to portray anything, and sometimes having a star is important. But there are plenty of situations that don't require a star. Besides there's probably a deaf Dustin Hoffman out there trying to get his first break.

"Knowing that people with disabilities can and want to work in this field made me excited about taking *Flavia* on the road," Clarke continues. "People could see actors with disabilties on a national tour in a technically complicated musical and find out they could do the work – that it was no big deal. They could see firsthand what we had produced together, away from all the restrictions everyone usually puts on things. We were each so different, but we made sacrifices for each other. We made the effort to be sure we were communicating and working as a team. And look what we accomplished together. We couldn't wait to tour."

—·—

Flavia and the Dream Maker never toured. Many theaters, hit by the recession of the early '90s, were saving money by booking one-man shows and small plays. There was

"I had been in a lot of shows, but *Flavia* was the first one I really wanted to do," remembers Noah Gaines. "The message was so cool and then Rod says 'stars are going to fall from the ceiling at the end,' and I'm like 'how are they going to do that?' It was magical."

Noah Gaines and Anne Jacoby

Flavia and the Dream Maker, Center Stage Theater, 1991

interest from Japan, but nothing materialized. The script was polished in anticipation of bookings that didn't come and a cast recording was made.

After almost a year of trying and waiting for dates, *Flavia* went on the back burner. Gerry Brady's light, ingenious set – so perfect for touring – was put away. Clarke went to Broadway with *Tommy*. Anne went on to the high school of performing arts in Los Angeles. C.J. took his one-man show on tour. Flavia's empire – and fan club – continued to grow, as the cast members went their separate ways to pursue their art.

"It was hard for all of us," Anne says, "because we believed in the show so much and wanted so much for it. And it had gone so far already on its dreams. We were clinging to this idea that we were gonna be together again. I was changing schools, I was changing a lot of things, and this was the one thing I really counted on, it was the thing that I had put all my hopes into. We waited and waited to get those tour dates. I desperately wanted to break away from eighth grade and just go with these people that I loved and share this wonderful experience with other people. Then the reality set in and I had to accept that we

weren't going to do it anymore. For awhile it was really difficult for me to find anything that fulfilled me the way Access Theatre did. Because nothing else could really compare. It was irreplaceable.

"I wish I could have known that night that it was going to be the last performance, " Anne says of the last show at Center Stage Theater. "It might have made it easier later on to let go. But instead we thought it was just the beginning. We had wonderful plans.

"Traditionally there's a final performance, so this was kind of anticlimactic. But I do remember something about that night. I remember I was singing "Touch the Sky," singing about missing Jack. From the ceiling there was a three-dimensional moon with stars spilling over it. I remember that particular night I looked up there at this cardboard moon and paper stars and I...I mean in my heart I really felt that the real Jack was really up there and really watching everything that we were doing.

"It was an eerie feeling that this show reached beyond what we were doing on stage. That what happened to Flavia was real, and things like that really do happen, and ultimately we're being watched over in some way.

In 1991, Access Theatre musician and actress Patty Neumeyer *(far left)* was cast in the CBS/Orion series *WIOU*, as a therapist who counsels co-star Dick Van Patten *(right, with director Bethany Rooney, center)* for his encroaching blindness.

"It was probably the funnest thing I've ever done," Patty recalls. They faxed up the script and Rod read it to me over my telephone answering machine so I could Braille it out for myself. Thom Rollerson went with me and stayed on the set to act as my manager; he just kept saying 'don't be stubborn. Be easy, be easy.'

"They were going to have me back for a second episode," Patty continues, "and Thom said 'don't say anything about the nudity until it's written.' Nudity! He said not to worry you'll wear body suits. And I told him 'I sing in church every Sunday, I can't be seen on TV wearing what everyone thinks is nothing.'

"The scene got written and it was definitely body suits and handcuffs and a hot scene in the bedroom. As a representative of my faith, I just *couldn't* do it. I prayed and I asked everyone I knew to pray. And CBS came in and toned the scene way down. I think it was because they felt that blind people should not be seen as sexpots and this was a bit too kinky, as if blind people do not have sex and do kinky things."

Between 1990 and 1994, Access Entertainment Services, organized and overseen by Thom Rollerson, secured work for several other Access Theatre performers. Robin Fortyune, who is quadriplegic, was cast with Martin Sheen and Annie Potts in a CBS television movie *My Dissident Mom*; developmentally disabled actress Sara Ostrowski was cast in a national AT&T commercial; and deaf comedian C.J. Jones was cast in an industrial video. Four Youth Access performers appeared in Melissa Manchester's 1990 music video for "Walk On By." Casey Pieretti, who lost a leg to a drunk driver, did TV's *Quantum Leap*, and deaf actors Billie Burke Perkins and John Maucere appeared in an NBC pilot, *Parker Kane*.

I felt very connected to this love for Jack and this love for someone who puts everything into perspective. I don't know how to describe it, it was like…seeing a way through. Do you know what I mean?"

Noah Gaines *(center)* in his solo "Man of the House"
with Michael Purcell, Clarke Thorell and C.J. Jones.
Flavia and the Dream Maker, Center Stage Theater, 1991

John Fink, Billie Burke Perkins and Val Limar

Listen for Wings!, 1992

winging it

She appeared one day in a colorful print scarf, brilliant white hair, and somewhat flashy pumps to volunteer as the office assistant. She would do anything, she explained, except answer phones, since she "actually couldn't hear a damn thing." She was a widow and a retired beautician, and she wanted to be an actress. "Like Billie Burke," she added with a grin, as if everyone had surely heard of the vaudeville queen she had been named after.

—·—

Billie Burke Perkins is nothing if not persistent. "In the dictionary, next to the word persistent…," Rod starts to say. Billie's other weapon is charm, that faultless combination of timing, bravado, and vulnerability that used to be called star quality. Like something out of a classic American musical, she continued to volunteer, ever-confident that all that stood between her and the stage was time. At last, in

1992, Rod asked award-winning playwright Ellen K. Anderson to write a new comedy around his Golden Volunteer who had won her chance to be a star.

"I remember the day I knew she would be fabulous to write for," Ellen says. "We were at the bowling alley for a company bachelor party. Billie had prepared a little striptease, only she was going to do it backwards. Someone said to me, 'your job is to play the kazoo while we bring in the stripper. She's waiting outside in a Cadillac.' So the lights go down and in walks Billie Burke Perkins with an old-fashioned camisole under her raincoat, and dresses herself in the bowling alley."

"The people in the other lanes stopped bowling," Billie remembers, "and they're shouting 'Take it off, take it off,' and Rod and Thom are shouting 'Put it on, put it on.'"

Ellen decided that Billie's play *Listen for Wings!*, would be about a fictional heroine based on Billie and incorporating stories from her life. Ellen got out her tape recorder, but Billie, who had begged long and hard for her big break, was suddenly a reluctant subject. "I was going to write a book about my life," she says, "so I kind of held back. But Rod said 'forget about the book, talk to Ellen.'"

Ellen collected hours of interviews and created the character of Nellie Melba Kelly, an ambitious white-haired deaf actress determined to get the lead in *Hello, Dolly!*. In the process Nellie drives her director, played by Rod, to exasperation, and gives two guardian angels a workout in backstage diplomacy.

"Artistically I needed to make it a fictional work, so I could get some distance and have control over the story," Ellen says, "but we were also making a vehicle for Billie – to make her look wonderful. We threw in a little soft shoe, a little piano playing. She got to cry, she got to dance, she got to tell jokes, she got to be herself in front of a lot of people.

"She is very simply a natural comedienne," Ellen concludes, "it's in her timing and in her sense of the outrageous. But it's also because, like all great comediennes, she has a certain poignancy. Some sad things have happened to her and that gives her a stature."

One night, years before, Billie's husband, and father of the couple's three daughters, came downstairs during the late news complaining that his arm hurt. Billie had read about heart attacks in the *Reader's Digest*. She bundled him into the car and headed for Santa Barbara Cottage Hospital. "Luckily there was no traffic," she says, "because it was pea soup fog. I had never driven with my husband in the car before, it felt so strange. Some angels were really with me because I never hit a red light." As they reached the hospital parking lot, he shifted on her shoulder, and began to speak. "But there were no lights, not even a streetlight," Billie says, "so I couldn't see his lips. Maybe he said I love you, maybe he said I'm sorry – I don't know. I will never know. It was too dark for me to hear him." She lifted him out of the car, honking the horn she couldn't hear. "They came running," she remembers, "but he had already died."

"She told me this while we were sitting stuffing envelopes for a newsletter mailing, with a little tear in her eye." Ellen remembers. "I had to go into the bathroom out of sight and fall apart.

(Front row left to right) Director Jenny Sullivan, playwright Ellen K. Anderson and
stage manager Kathleen Parsons with cast, *Listen for Wings!*, 1992

"They were all 100% there for Billie," says director Jenny Sullivan.
"They really understood about ensemble and about supporting Billie to
be the star. In television and even on stage, I haven't always seen
that kind of generosity from actors."

"It was dramatic and it was real, and that's why it had to be in the play," Ellen says of the story, one of several tales from Billie's life woven into *Listen for Wings!*. The idea, Ellen says, was to balance the comedy with a spice of drama – to conjure a side of Billie beyond the entertainer she had so carefully cultivated over the years.

———

Billie Burke Perkins will not tell her age, will not even hint at it. "I don't remember dates," she will say to close the subject. She started to become deaf when she was in elementary school, but never learned sign language, though she did learn to play the piano and sing a little. Her husband courted her at their friends' parties all over Santa Barbara and she was considered a good dancer. "But I don't like to brag," she quickly adds. Billie is proud, manipulative, and utterly sincere, and her ambition pours out of her in a way that should be infuriating but isn't. She tends to put a good face on things, because she wants to be popular, because she doesn't want to be relegated to the background of life.

"In school, as my hearing got worse, to get more people to like me I would do funny things to make people laugh," Billie remembers, but the strategy didn't always work. "With the kids at school, if you can't hear you're stupid. That's just the way it is. Being deaf turns people off. If people know you are deaf, they say you can't do things," she continues, "and I wanted to do things. Mostly, I liked doing things where I could be seen. To sum it all up, I was kind of the life of the party. It was always 'ask Billie, she'll tell something funny.' So before I would go out, I'd think in my mind what I was going to say and have it all mapped out. I'd be ready."

As deaf pride and culture emerged, as younger deaf people gradually asserted their civil rights and identity, Billie remained very much of her generation. Just as she would never leave the house without looking her best, and is slow to tell her secrets, she preferred to pass for hearing.

"Billie has probably spent a lot of her life saying I'm fine, I'm OK," says director Jenny Sullivan. A television and stage director, Jenny came home to Santa Barbara to guest direct *Wings* and mend from an exhausting journey to Broadway with one of her best known directorial projects, Jane Anderson's play *The Baby Dance*.

"She reminded me so much of my

Billie and George

mother who is also a very vivid person," Jenny says. "Mom was an MGM contract player who all but gave up her career to be Mrs. Barry Sullivan, movie star wife. Billie's spirit reminded me of her, the 'hey look me over I'm a babe' attitude. They both are very sexual beings – showoffs – and could get away with it. They really *love* people, they love to dance. They're party girls. They have strong opinions about things and people; they're protective of their family. The few times I saw Billie's feelings get hurt it reminded me of how my mom's feelings could get hurt. It was devastating because you didn't see it very often. They both have strong facades in terms of being the up, larger than life person.

"Finding Billie's dark side, the sad side, was a challenge, finding the path into that part of her was hard. Because she, like my mother, has spent a long time presenting herself, saying 'this is who I am in the world and the rest is very private.'

"I think we all went into this project with an emotional sense of Billie's nerve, tenacity, power, outrageousness, guts," Ellen says. "She gave me a real sense of why she deserved to have a play of her own. I admired her enough to do that work, and it's a huge amount of work."

Every night, after rehearsals, Billie would ask Rod to stay and run scenes. Over and over. Sometimes until 1:30 a.m. Most mornings Rod went back to the hospital where his mother was desperately ill. Billie would go home, only to be up again at 4 a.m., practicing in front of her bedroom mirror.

Billie had to memorize the whole play, everybody's lines, because she would never actually hear them spoken. Billie, who loves Sid Caesar, Mickey Rooney, and Jerry Seinfeld, also had to learn about acting, not just performing. "She's a star," Jenny says, "She knew how to be an entertainer. We worked to get at another level, to get her to dig into her personal self."

"I would actually take her part and show her how I would deliver her line," Rod says. "That's normally a real no-no, but with her that was OK, because she couldn't help but make things her own." Ellen would come to rehearsals and rewrite a phrase, a bridge, even a scene as needed. "More lines to learn, all the time," Billie groans.

"Comedy is hard," Jenny says, "it's a finely tuned kind of instrument. If you're going

Michael Douglas and company, *Listen for Wings!*, 1992

for tragedy you can use a much broader palette. When you go for comedy it's very precise and somewhat indescribable. This was a comedy where the actress wouldn't hear the audience laugh, so there were all kinds of timing issues. Billie's got her own timing. So she's got her own comedy. We had to make that work into the whole picture."

"On stage with Rod, a lot of times his character was looking at me and I could read his lips to know when to say my line," Billie says. But John Fink and Val Limar played invisible guardian angels – Billie could not look at them to read their lips. "It was embarrassing because I cut in on my angel John Fink and he didn't get to finish his sentence," Billie remembers, horrified at her breach of professional courtesy. "I apologized so much because I would *never* do that intentionally,"

So they came up with hundreds of little cues to let Billie know when to say her lines. John might touch her shoulder; the sign language interpreter, Katie Voice, might wink at her. Rod might start writing with his pencil, or finish a line just as he reached a predetermined landmark on the stage.

It was a lot to remember. Sometimes Billie would skip ahead in the text, an easy

thing to do when you are not hearing other people's lines. And once Billie actually "went up" – forgot her lines. "Luckily my character was sitting at the desk writing," Rod remembers, "so I just started writing her lines on the paper and subtly sliding it over to her, and kind of gesturing with my head to get her to look down and read it. It was a little tricky because my character was supposed to be ignoring her at the time, and she had to read it upside down."

"That cast had to be more responsible as an ensemble," Jenny says. "They were responsible for helping Billie do her job, and they all, including Billie, had to be responsible for sight lines, to keep the interpreter in view for deaf audience members."

"Jenny was directing in two languages," Rod says, "one of which had to be seen rather than heard. The audience had to see the interpreter, and I was also signing nearly all of my lines. The same way you would not want an actor to mumble or speak upstage, our hands and faces had to be clearly visible at all times."

"We were just enveloped in so many elements," Jenny says. "We had angels who were supposed to be invisible, people speaking, people signing, people cueing Billie. At times I felt like I was directing three plays at once."

But Billie's deafness also worked to the director's advantage. "Rod was having a hard time," Jenny says, "because his character had to be really mean to Billie, which was totally unnatural for Rod. So when he wasn't looking I would mouth instructions to Billie without using my voice, to get her to try things that might take him by surprise, or help draw his character out." "Like 'pretend you're seducing him,' and things like that." Billie adds.

"Ironically, I talked more, and used more words, on that play than anything else I've ever directed," Jenny continues. "With Billie I couldn't do the shorthand you get in the habit of doing with more experienced actors, who understand a grunt or an uhhhh. I had to be very specific with her. Very literal. I had to be careful with idiom, careful of the expressions I used. At the end of the day my mouth would hurt, from straining to be clear in my speech."

After rehearsals, the actors huddled around the laptop computer so Jenny could type the daily notes – "things we could improve on," Billie says. "It would be Billie... Billie... Billie again. I said 'doesn't Rod ever do anything wrong?' and Jenny said 'yes I have a few things for him.' So that made me happy that he did something wrong too, but I still had ten times more things."

"If you see the character fully developed in the first rehearsal you're in trouble," Jenny says of the arduous but rewarding process, "because you have no place to go.

"I got to create something with Billie. We got to discover it to the best of *our* ability together in a collaboration.

"She was a piece of cake to work with because she was so completely willing. To me, the dream actors are the ones who will go for it, who will try what you ask them to do. You can tell that actors are going to be a pain in the ass when 'no' is the first word that comes out of their mouth. That's much more deadly than being inexperienced. Or deaf."

———

Listen for Wings! toured successfully throughout Wyoming and California. Billie loved the traveling, the hotels, the audiences, and the roses at her curtain call. She got to meet her idol George Burns. Michael Douglas came to see her backstage. Joel Schumacher – director of the *Batman* sequels – saw the show twice and told Billie he'd put her in a movie one day. She's still waiting.

"She was starring in a full length play for the first time in her entire life," Ellen says, "so she had undertaken a huge piece of work. And when we started no one knew for sure that she could do it."

"At first I didn't understand how wonderful it was," Billie says. "I never thought 'this is my own play all about me,' I was just working too hard. But I enjoy trying to prove things. I don't like people to say you can't do this or that because you can't hear. Well how do you know? I didn't think about not being able to do it. I thought I *am* going to do it. You have to make up your mind if you want something, you can't just sit down and wait for someone to come along and put their arm around you. You just do it, whatever it is you have to do.

"I wanted to go on the stage so bad I would have done anything," Billie adds, "just like Nellie. Except I wouldn't ruin someone's life, like she did to her director. But I would do *almost* anything. I like to make people laugh, I like the adulation and all the clapping. If you can get up there and tell some jokes and entertain people, they aren't going to think about you being deaf."

"The rewards were so great," Ellen says.

"People stood up for her. Rooms full of people stood up for her. They genuinely admired her work, genuinely admired her nerve."

"I always had a feeling I would get this play one way or another," Billie says. "because I really, really wanted it. I think I wanted it more than I wanted to hear. That's a terrible thing to say. But it's true."

Billie Burke Perkins and John Fink

Listen for Wings!, Center Stage Theater, 1992

"She's a strong presence," says playwright Ellen K. Anderson.

"She's cooking on all burners. I don't think she's got a lot of down time around people."

Judson Morgan, *Godspell*, Garvin Theatre Complex, 1994

a new generation

Judson Morgan stood on a grassy hill at Santa Barbara City College squinting into the hot sun and feeling sorry for himself. This was definitely not his idea of a rehearsal. The 15-year-old actor and singer had just been cast in his dream role – Jesus in *Godspell*. But at the moment, the dream was stalled over sign language, two *hours* of sign language, before the "real" rehearsal could begin.

Interpreter Michael Purcell drilled the cast. His gestures were crisp as he stressed the subtleties of the language to his young acolytes. Jud wished he were someplace else.

"I'll just tell them," he thought to himself. "I'll tell them I'm not signing and that's that. I'll explain that I need the time for my singing and my acting, that the sign is ruining everything. They'll just have to understand." As it would turn out, Jud was the one who didn't yet understand.

Godspell was the 1994 summer youth musical, part of Access Theatre's Youth Access to the Arts program. Under director Peter McCorkle and technical director Tal Sanders, the teens were spending the summer getting real production experience, putting their mark on one of theater's war-horses, the 1972 Tebelak/Schwartz musical *Godspell*. The production was sprinkled with contemporary gags: Jesus was baptized with a loofa, there were references to Julia Child, *Charlie's Angels* and *Beavis and Butthead*. They were making it young and fun.

But the young actors were also getting a glimpse of something more. Working alongside deaf cast member Sarah Peterson, and with Michael's determined sign instruction, they were getting a chance to see what accessibility in theater could mean. They were learning how to rise above a good performance and achieve a more universal one.

"I actually thought I had enough pull to

say I'm not doing the signing," Jud remembers with a laugh. "When Michael was rehearsing us I was like 'whatever,' just tuning it out. I knew that wasn't a great attitude, but I just wasn't interested. I didn't even want the interpreter to be near me on stage.

"And then something happened – and I know exactly when it happened. Michael showed us what I would be doing for the song "God Save the People." One of the signs just killed me – it was the sign when the sun comes up over the clouds – and when he did that I kinda got chills. Seriously. And I was like 'whoa, that is so beautiful and that communicates so well' and after that I started sayin' to myself, 'this is gonna be really special.' I started telling people, 'you gotta come see this.'

"See at first I was just interested in my *acting*, I wanted to act the part as well and truthfully as I could and I felt like the sign language was going to detract from that. And for awhile it does, for a long time it's really inhibiting. But there's a point when you definitely take hold of it and you can *start* to use it as a tool. For me it opened up a lot of new muscles, and got my body more involved. Michael was always telling us to breathe and bend our

knees and flow with it. It made it more like life was a dance, instead of life was these choppy little sentences and songs.

"The sign language helped us to think about what we were saying, know what we were saying, feel it, and kind of give it from the heart. Because when you're signing, you're moving out and saying 'here, this is me, and here is my body, and I'm not just saying these words, I'm committed. I'm fully here and I'm fully here for *you*.' It made me more vulnerable to myself and to the audience, and to other actors. It made me more open to being humble and truthful in my performance

"After a few weeks, I kind of realized something else. I realized that if Jesus had come today like we were portraying in *Godspell*, He would have totally known sign language and He would have been using it. The idea that anyone's left out wouldn't be right for Him. That made it very real for me. It was like He was there for all people, and we were trying to be too. No matter whether a deaf person was in the audience that night or not. It was about including everybody. And you know, that inclusion – it's as good as everyone says it is.

"The feeling that we are all on this

"High spirits...the
exuberance and vitality of
youth harnessed to a
definite and constructive
goal," observed the *Santa
Barbara Independent* critic.

Cast, "Finale," *Godspell*,
Garvin Theatre Complex,
1994

Joyce Kondak, Judson Morgan and Tori Lewis with
Aaron Levin and Michael Purcell, "By My Side,"
Godspell, Garvin Theatre Complex, 1994

plateau, we are all human, we are all created equal, it's in *action* at Access. It's not like they say it, they talk about it, maybe they do a piece of theater about it. It's happening; it's actually happening. And it's like our humanness is our offering to the audience.

"I think it's inspiring. I think it's *shocking*. People come into that theater to see a play, and they see something about *themselves* – they have a life experience. They didn't count on that.

"I feel like it gets into people's hearts and into their bodies and into their muscles instead of into their brains. It changes people without their meaning to be changed when they see some truth that they haven't heard or seen before. The truth gets to people. I know it gets to me."

—·—

Tyler Dumm lost his eyesight to cancer before he was two years old, but fills his life with roller blades, bicycles, soccer, video games and Lego. In 1991, when he was 8 years old, he was out horseback riding when he met Access Theatre's company manager Thom Rollerson. Thom convinced him to try out for a small part in the company's production of *At

Long Last Leo. Tyler was cast and immediately became absorbed by the theater, learning to use the backstage monitor to catch his cues, and thinking on his feet when someone dropped a line. In a cast full of grownups, of Equity actors and well-known TV stars, he fit right in.

The following year, Tyler started taking acting classes as part of Access Theatre's Young Performers Workshop with storyteller and actress Nadja Forest. As part of the program, Nadja, Rod, and playwright Ty Granaroli developed an original play, *In-Sight*, in collaboration with the fifth-graders in the cast.

"We talked a lot about school," Tyler says, "what people say, and what the cool things are. What the bad things are. How people treat other kids. We combined all our ideas into a script. My idea was something I hated in school – people would say to me 'how many fingers am I holding up?' They included it. We were all thinking of things we hated. Like the kids tease Camille 'cause her last name's Kitchen and they tease Daniel cause he's short or they tease Noah 'cause he's Noah's Ark.

"Or like how it feels when people ask other people questions about me that I could

"An unforgettable experience," one Santa Barbara teacher wrote of *In-Sight*. "I cannot recall seeing such an appropriate and meaningful experience at this school in 25 years."

Tyler Dumm and Daniel Seward
In-Sight, 1993

"I thought this was just the worst idea in the world to tour it to the schools, because I was going to get made fun of for the rest of my life," says Noah Gaines *(center)*. "But it was actually pretty good." "Like it says in the play, there's a lot of different ways to be cool," adds Camille Kitchen *(far right)* with Tyler Dumm, Debbie Daniel, Daniel Seward *(top)* and Elizabeth Heller, *In-Sight*, 1993

203

answer perfectly myself. Like 'does he read? How does he do his homework?' It's like 'gee you can ask *me*!'

"That's what the script was based on, and also good things too. They'd ask us questions and we'd tell about experiences. Ty wrote all this down and the next time he came he had a little bit of a script. Sometimes he'd word it from an adult's point of view, so we helped fix that. And after awhile he understood. He started to get more like a kid.

"The play was about how kids react to people with disabilities, and that disabilities are not just physical like you can't see or you have cerebral palsy. Everybody has a disability, you know; there's nobody that is perfect. Like Noah's character had a disability because he was a bully, and Debbie had a disability, she was shy. Daniel had a kind of disability, he was supposedly a nerd, and if people made fun of him he just took it. So that was the message, that there are all kinds of disabilities."

In-Sight toured in the schools through spring of 1993 to enthusiastic reaction from young audiences and educators. "This is a stunning piece of work," came a letter from one administrator, "our students, staff and parents were moved from laughter to tears."

More performances were planned, and canceled when Tyler developed a fast-moving cancer in his left leg and went into a year of tough treatment. It was a big disappointment for the whole cast, and especially for Tyler – who now pronounces his cancer "99.9%" gone. He continues to cycle and rollerblade, breaking in his prosthetic leg in the new world of junior high school.

"It was a good play and it has a good message," he says now from his 13-year-old vantage point. "It told people what it is like, and what it *could* be like. That everybody has a disability, maybe not a physical one, but you're just different, you're always different from other people in some way. So the only way to get to know about people is to give 'em time to see what they're really like.

"I think most people make decisions on looks, about a lot of things, not just about people. Like on a high dive, people who can see look down and think 'oh man that's *really* far and I don't know if I can do that.' Now I don't know how far down it is, do I? So I jump, hit the water, swim to the side and do it again. I like it. If I happen to flip over four times and hit the water on my back then I don't like it. It's the *experience* that matters.

When staff members of the National Council on Alcoholism, first saw Access Theatre perform, they had an idea. Why not commission the company to produce a new musical aimed at substance abuse among teens? "I thought we could present a new and different approach," says Judy Hearsum, then assistant executive director of the council. "A lot of people, especially younger people are turned off by 'traditional' approaches. They can see right through them."

After meeting with counselors and members of Alcoholics Anonymous and Alateen, it was clear that such a production would suit Access Theatre's charter, even though it did not deal specifically with disability. As it turned out, Rod was able to cast one actor, Steven Ferguson who uses a wheelchair and Marnee Wafer who is hard of hearing. Fran Buker's sign language interpretation insured accessibility for deaf audience members.

Most importantly, the show had Davida Wills' realistic script, the hard-driving Mark Henderson/Eddie Glickman songs, and the clear, true voices of a strong cast, including budding rock star Tiffany Renee. Like most Access Theatre shows, the combination of realistic dialogue and an optimistic compassion for people's differences hit the mark with audiences.

205

In school tours through 1985 and 1986, *Olly Olly Oxen Free* drew laughter and cheers, and serious feedback in post-performance discussions. "One 14-year-old boy said he knew after seeing the play that if he didn't get help, he'd be dead in a week," Rod recalls. "When people walked out of that show they had a lot to think about, and more than that they were *open* to thinking about it. They hadn't been beat over the head, and hopefully they had been given an idea of how they might solve a problem in real life."

Steven Ferguson, Marnee Wafer, Tiffany Renee and Ann Bengry *(front row)*,
Joi Martins, Russell Ricard, Brian Sullivan and Stephen Kay *(back row)*, *Olly Olly Oxen Free*, 1986

"I remember people by the experience of them too. Like when I think of my friend Ian, I don't see an image, he's just whole. It's what I remember about him, like when we were running through the woods in first grade, or how it feels when we're together getting ready to catch a wave, with his arm over me holding me into the wave. People don't 'look' any way to me, they're just there. They're an experience.

"The play was kind of about that. That you can't know about a person just by looking at them and deciding – that's a nerd, that's a bully. Yeah, you can tell *some* things about a person just by looking at them. You can get a physical description like 'oh, that kid has a pointy nose,' He probably does have a pointy nose and he'd admit it, but that's all you get. You can't get bully or nerd.

"It's like there could be this ingenious guy who could make space ships that could go four thousand million light years away and find this different planet, and he can be totally ugly, like he has warts all over his face and he's pale, and people think 'Ugh, he's never going to do anything good. Just throw him out.' That could be a big mistake. Some people think by – judge by – what they see. That's OK for some things. But you don't do that to people."

Access Theatre began working with youth from the very first production in 1979. Over the years, the company toured most of its shows to schools throughout the western states, and offered ongoing workshops and special performances for youth audiences. In 1994, the focus on youth expanded under a new name, "Youth Access to the Arts."

Peter McCorkle, a 15-year Access veteran, dancer, and choreographer, was hired as Youth Director. He joined long-time Access instructor Nadja Forest and a group of multi-talented teachers in the new program.

Under the company's program director Daniel Girard, Peter and staff organized multi-disciplinary workshops offering classes in performance and technical skills. The program also offered real production experience, on stage and behind the scenes. The goal was to give students quality training, and help them learn to be better communicators regardless of their theatrical aspirations. New funding came from city, county and state agencies, and from local businesses and foundations. A grant from the John Percival and Mary C. Jefferson Endowment and the Weingart Foundation,

Tyler Dumm (Mad Hatter),
Daniel Seward (White Rabbit),
and members and staff of
Access Theatre's "Experience
the Arts" Workshop, Summer
Solstice Parade, 1991

One of Clark Sayre's goals when he returned home to Santa Barbara from Broadway in the early '90s was to start a young playwrights workshop and festival. Students in his 4-year-old Access Theatre program ranged in age from 12 to 21 and each were paired with a mentor — professionals including Ellen Anderson, Robert Potter, and Lily Wong. Guest speakers included filmmaker Bob Zemeckis (*Forrest Gump*) and screenwriters Peter Seamen and Jeffrey Price *(all pictured with students above)*. The students' one act plays were given full production in a weekend-long festival, now an annual event. "I wanted to see young people create theater, rather than just act in theater," Clark says, "Because their unique voices are important."

among others, supported scholarships. It all helped fulfill a personal dream that Rod had been working towards for a long time – to give youth the kind of access to the stage he had enjoyed himself.

Rod, Peter, and Clark Sayre, who founded the company's Young Playwright's Workshop, all grew up in Santa Barbara with rich theatrical opportunities at local public schools and in summer programs with Santa Barbara Youth Theatre. These opportunities had shaped their lives, and those of other young people, including ER's Anthony Edwards, Clare Carey of Coach, film actor Eric Stoltz, entertainment executives Gary Goddard and Tony Christopher, Broadway stars Howard McGillan and Cady Huffman, and dozens of others who went on to work in stage, television, and film, as performers, writers, directors, and musicians.

In the '90s, opportunities for youth were no longer so plentiful, and Rod and company were eager to fill the void. They also found out that young actors of this generation didn't just want to do musical comedy, they wanted something with relevance to their lives – they wanted a voice.

In 1994, Ty Granaroli, author of In-Sight,

went to work on a play for teens, planned for school tours. The new play tackled a complex environmental issue, a topical and controversial subject in Santa Barbara.

But when Ty, Rod and co-director Nadja Forest went into the schools to audition for the work in progress, they found that the students had very different issues on their minds. Though it had been months in development, the first script was scrapped and Ty spent an intense two weeks writing a tough, contemporary drama. Stix and Stonz was about a shooting at a high school and the reaction, conflicts, and cautious peacemaking of a bunch of kids cooped up together to wait for adults to decide what to do.

"Even though it's Santa Barbara, and a small, reasonably safe town, we found out that this was what kids were really thinking about," Nadja says. "We had made this commitment to give young people a voice, and to be accessible to youth. This was what came up, so to me, that's what you write about."

To formulate the characters, Ty interviewed the young actors, as well as a former gang member. His story revolves around what happens when a group of teens – a tagger, a nerd, a gang member, a feminist, a goody-

goody, an idealist, and a shy bystander – are thrown together and left to sort things out among themselves. Though it was sign language interpreted, *Stix and Stonz* was not specifically about disability. It expanded on a common Access theme – breaking down the differences among people who, despite appearances, may not be so different after all. Most significantly to the kids, Ty used their own stories and fears to inspire the drama, and let the characters say the words they would use in real life.

"I hate to overemphasize it, but the language let people know this was for real," says Devon Colin, who played the gangbanger and catalyst for the drama. "At the moment when things started getting real we didn't say 'coca-doody,' or 'I don't freakin' like this, this is dookie,' but said 'this is *bullshit*, man.' That's when the audience thinks, 'whoa they're not messin' around, they're gonna tell this how it is.'"

A few schools refused the show because of the language and what they considered volatile subject matter. But the administrators that took the show found to their surprise that kids listened in assembly and often spoke candidly in the talkback dialogues afterwards. *Stix and Stonz* had captured the students' fickle attention where other assemblies had not.

"It's scary to go up in front of a school audience sometimes," remembers David Aumentado, who played a quiet tagger. "You're looking out at them and you can tell by the way they're sitting and their body language they're like 'oh no, another play' and maybe they're making fun of us or something. So they start out with this attitude. Then the play starts getting more intense, and that's when we knew they were really listening. I think it was because it was so real.

"It was about something that is everywhere around us. I don't think you need to be subject to gang violence to feel this. I've seen violence, I've seen domestic violence, and I mean *that's* violent. You don't need to see somebody get shot to know what violence is.

"I could have written a play without them," Ty says. "But it wouldn't have been as honest. They had an incredible amount of input into the script, they were listened to and participated in a way that a lot of actors, even adult actors don't get to. Every kid had a chance to say, 'I wouldn't say this, I wouldn't get up and cross the room here, will you change this line?' But they didn't always get their way, sometimes we pushed them to stretch and go after a character that wasn't

In the summer of 1995, Access Theatre's Youth Access to the Arts hit a peak with *Leap!* The musical was written, produced, performed, and run by a multi-generational team of Access company artists and members of the youth program. "A strong cast, soulful songs, and a passion for performance," praised *Santa Barbara Independent* critic Paul Froemming.

Rod had not initially planned to do an original piece. All spring, the staff read published scripts. They finally abandoned the search and took a calculated risk — they would create a new musical specifically for the young cast. It turned out to be a massive undertaking that culminated in two weeks of successful performances in the theater at Santa Barbara High School, Rod's alma mater.

Ty Granaroli, who wrote the company's youth dramas *In-Sight* and *Stix and Stonz*, based his contemporary script for *Leap!* on interviews with the young actors. In the playwright's words, the teens "live in a world that seems to be getting harder to figure out by the minute" so the writing sought to address the fears of young people disabled by apathy and anxiety. Directed by Rod and Nadja Forest, the show's fable-like story follows the adventures and awakening of a young, angst-ridden outsider named Jack in his conflicts with parents, peers, and life.

Lyricist Johnny Elkins and composers Mark Henderson and Greg Kuhn created the emotional, pop-influenced songs. Designer Tal Sanders' impressive set — one of Access Theatre's most ambitious and difficult — combined a high tech, video-inspired set, with sophisticated MTV-style visual effects. All this technology represents the information overload that drives Jack on his own inward journey into "The Gap." There, Jack meets the Innocent — his younger, wiser self.

Interpreter Michael Purcell, with intern interpreter Megan Lee, wove sign language into the highly visual show. They even incorporated it into choreography — for example in the highly effective scene "Hang Time" featuring Jack's dropout friends, the Slackers *(above right)*. Program Director Daniel Girard coordinated the other accessibility services, including audio description for people who are blind, open captioning, assistive listening, and Spanish translation. *Leap!* drew on sixteen years of the company's experience with accessible theater and creating original work. In every aspect of the production, adult leaders used interns from the youth program. Young participants could have their pick of disciplines from stage carpentry to box office to sign language interpretation for the stage.

Gioia Marchese,
Michael Peacock,
Tobias Jelinek,
Jon Rickman,
Judson Morgan,
Holly Ferguson,
Michael Gonzales,
Laurie Gold, and
Quinn Gonzales,
Leap!, 1995

Judson Morgan as
Jack and Austin
McCormick as The
Innocent with
interpreter Michael
Purcell, *Leap!*, 1995

comfortable at first. Many times the words they objected to were words they had actually said in the interviews. So it was partly a matter of getting them to see themselves and draw on what was real, not just an idealized idea of what they wanted to be."

"It's hard for me to play this role," Devon admits. "First of all I used to think I was like that, right, all hard and all. I got outta that and this play brings that back. So I have to laugh at myself, and naturally I don't like laughing at myself. It was a hard part. But you get a lot of help with the characterization from the directors. It's more personal, they actually care about us, we're not just meat that goes through their classroom."

"I learned how to focus and listen," adds David, "as well as basic acting skills, like enunciation and projection. Also how to dig deep into your inner self and find what will make the character real. Sometimes that was hard for all of us. I remember Josh was having trouble getting angry in his part. Rod took him outside with a chair and a broom and had him reciting his lines while he was whacking the heck out of a chair with a broomstick. Just doing it over and over. And when he came back in for a group rehearsal he just tore Devon up.

"Everyone in this play has to have the courage to do it or it won't work" David continues." For me, if I did a good job my stomach will be shot, and my throat will be raw, and my eyes will be wide open. I'll just know that I put all that I could into it. If I know I did the best I could and the audience is like 'yeah I understood it,' then that's good."

"But it's not enough," Devon adds. "I think we need to touch everybody or everybody needs to touch something in themselves. Because for every person who may understand what we're trying to say there's three people that are sayin' 'you know, just go away.' I know 'cause I was like that. I was negative. I said 'why does it matter, dude, none of this matters.' But you know what – it does matter. I guess you could say I've gone from negative to just pessimistic.

"As far as changing things with one play, I don't know because frankly it takes everybody to change anything. I don't believe one person can change the world, because when that person's gone everybody sits down again. Still...if I could know that I touched one person, if somebody came up to me and said, 'you really touched me dude'... that would be the greatest thing. I think everybody wants to hear that."

"It's *work*. It feels good in the same way that pounding nails and lifting wood and

getting physically tired does. It wears you out, but you know you're *doing* something,"

Devon Colin with Ben Provo and David Aumentado, *Stix and Stonz*, 1994

—·—

"These kids had a chance to make themselves heard and make themselves satisfied with the product," says playwright Ty Granaroli. "Rod builds a situation where everybody is collaborating. He decides to listen to input. Most people don't have the confidence to let work happen that way because it can become chaos. He makes the decision not to be still and rigid. It's a supple process. It's respect."

"It's alive theater," says Judson Morgan. "It's not about 'look how well we pose' or even 'look how wise and clever we are.' Hopefully it's about 'here is my offering, here is *me* and a piece of my life.' It helped me understand theater not just as a display of talent, but showing lives and insights. It's so valuable just to see some truth in another person, and then compare it to your life, add it to your life and say 'now I can grow up a little bit higher, now I can grow one more branch.' Access Theatre says that people with disabilities have as much to add to that as anyone else and so do young people.

"We weren't just a bunch of kids; we were people who had lived a life, and whatever that was – it was shorter than Rod's or Peter's or Nadja's – but we had 15 years of experience. They have more years of experience. But 15 years is a lot, and our lives have meaning, and Access Theatre gave us a chance to bring that out."

"I think it's hard for people to listen sometimes," says *Stix and Stonz* cast member Nora Lange. "This play is a mirror image of what they do, but they don't listen to themselves, they don't want to hear themselves, hear how they sound when they put someone down. If they want to learn, if they want to listen, this show can help change their views, or add on to their views and help them make their own decisions about what they will and will not do. I think it's good information."

Geren Piltz, Maria Goena, and Devon Colin

Stix and Stonz, 1994

On **funding**

and Support

Three important policies shaped Access Theatre's financial life and remained constant throughout the history of the company. First – and most unusual for an arts organization – the company operated in the black for 18 years. Second, volunteer help and in-kind donations of goods or services remained a crucial form of support, even as grants and cash gifts grew to provide the bulk of the budget.

Ultimately, the policy that most influenced the course of Access Theatre's development was collaboration. Rod sought and responded to propositions that joined the company with agencies such as the County Water Districts and the local Council on Alcoholism, as well as other arts organizations. From the earliest shows on, Access Theatre worked with a wide range of partners, often in innovative ways. These collaborations helped to insure the financial health of the company and define Access Theatre's role in the community. The big financial picture for Access Theatre indicates something so important that it is impossible to quantify on a balance sheet. Every $5 donation, every gift of goods and services, every collaborative project broadened community investment in the company, and that translated into reputation and audience.

This kind of support happened in part because Rod was a local boy – a fourth generation Santa Barbaran with a family that was well-established in the business community. Rod built on these connections, and created his own, until countless businesses donated everything from foam rubber to catering to assistive listening devices for audience members. Even after Access Theatre became an international touring company, the advertising and promotion donated by the *Santa Barbara Independent* and local radio stations, for example, remained a significant annual contribution to the budget.

Though the lion's share of funding came from grants and the generosity of key individuals, and though Access Theatre ultimately built an endowment, at no time could Rod simply write checks for everything. Every budget was a pastiche of sources, drawing on in-kind donations, ticket sales, and the collective power of small gifts from individuals. Every show was financed with a new twist, even as budgets grew from $3000 for *Circus of Life* to $150,000 for *Flavia and the Dream Maker* to the $500,000 for *Flight* which was never fully raised.

———

It seems appropriate that some of Access Theatre's early funding came – literally – from Santa Claus. Picture Rod Lathim – underpaid theater artist, blessed with twinkling blue eyes and apple cheeks. Four weeks of full-time Santa jobs paid much of his living expenses, and left him free to spend the rest of the year as a hand-to-mouth producer/director.

The $3000 budget for the first show, *Circus of Life*, came largely from the City of Santa Barbara Recreation Department and the Joseph P. Kennedy Foundation. But nearly as important, paint for the scenery came from local retailer Atens Ameritone, and volunteers sewed, chauffeured, chaperoned, and composed the music. Proceeds from ticket sales – about $2000 – were donated to Special Olympics, so the developmentally disabled actors were not just on the receiving end of donations, they were giving back to their own community.

The second show, *Through Our Eyes*, was also produced in cooperation with the Santa Barbara Recreation Department with a grant from the Association for Retarded Citizens. The balance of the $7000 budget came from Sambo's restaurants, when Rod asked owner and fellow Santa Barbaran Sam Battistone for the funds. The show's playbill – produced through donated graphics design and printing – featured paid advertising from local businesses ranging from a plumber to a beauty salon to the Nautilus Fitness Center, Rod's gym. Over 100 sponsors were thanked in print – including local individuals, a pharmacy, a state senator, a bowling alley, and Rod's bank. Each one represented a phone call or a letter from Rod, his parents, or a company member asking for help.

"We started by asking the businesses we patronized," Rod recalls, "and we got more aggressive about seeking support. We knew we

Michael McDonald, longtime company
supporter Kenny Loggins, and Santa (Rod),
at the Santa Barbara Rehabilitation Institute,
1984. In addition to receiving funding, Access
Theatre donated talent to other fundraising
efforts for organizations including United
Cerebral Palsy, UCSB affiliates, Multiple
Sclerosis, Special Olympics and the local
AIDS hospice Heath House.

needed it from our shoestring experience with *Circus of Life*. I didn't mind asking people, I was really excited about it then – first-time asks were a lot easier than tenth-time. In those days $50 went a long way – and it's much easier to ask for $50 than $500."

In 1980, Rod took a serious step that would open his eyes to the difficulties and importance of funding as a full time part of his job. Santa Barbara's Independent Living Resource Center (ILRC), a service and advocacy organization for people with disabilities, invited the company under its funding umbrella. Access Theatre would automatically receive non-profit status under the ILRC's 501(c)(3); the ILRC would take care of bookkeeping for a fee of 7% of the funds Rod raised for the theater.

In return, with Access Theatre's donations on its books, the ILRC's total cash base would increase, making it eligible for larger matching grants from state social service agencies. The ILRC would also have a powerful ambassador in the highly visible theater company, and would see its name associated with shows through 1988.

"We stayed with the ILRC about three years too long," Rod says now. "The reason was simply comfort. I was content not to have to deal with the details of the 501(c)(3), the bookkeeping and paperwork. I didn't have to maintain a formal board. But we could have done better faster if we had been on our own."

The first two shows produced under the ILRC arrangement were supported with grants from the City of Santa Barbara Promotional Funds, the company's first government money. The shows were also funded in part through an innovative arrangement with Santa Barbara City College Continuing Education. Rehearsals were offered as an adult education class, and Rod was paid a modest salary to teach the class. This solution also took care of an ever-present problem for the young company: rehearsal space.

At this time Rod also began a long-standing relationship with the Lobero Theatre Foundation and director Nancy Moore. The Lobero's support allowed the company to use the historic theater at a discounted rate. Rod and Nancy also wrote grants for joint projects. Years later, Rod helped the Lobero implement its $75,000 accessibility renovation to bring the 120-year-old theater closer to compliance with Assembly Bill 504 and the impending Americans With Disabilities Act.

By the time Access Theatre's sign language revue, *Signing Off*, was mounted in 1981, the company's budget was about $20,000 – nearly seven times the budget for *Circus of Life*. The California Arts Council was supporting the company, as was a state program called Area IX Developmental Disabilities Board – an experimental program to fund new projects for people with developmental disabilities. "They gave us $22,000," Rod remembers, "which to me was like $22 million, and boy did I make it last."

———

"I wrote grants and most of them got denied. And I learned from that," Rod remembers. "In 1981 and '82, we were growing and spending more on shows. We needed substantial money – not just $100 at a time. The Fund for Santa Barbara was the first foundation to gamble on us. But our short track record and my lack of experience in writing grants were hard to overcome."

Rod's early grant applications were full of the passion and worthiness of his cause and short on the details that sway most foundations. "There's an art to grant writing. It's not about emotions. You've got to be really objective and analytical about what you're going to do, how you're going to do it and how you will measure your success. Another hurdle for us, in the beginning, was that accessible performing arts was still a novelty – was it therapeutic or was it art? A lot of art funding entities didn't want to fund therapy.

"You have to understand exactly what a funder is interested in supporting," Rod continues, "because most have very specific guidelines. If you're not a match, they will turn you down." Ironically, though this was usually true, one of Access Theatre's most loyal supporters was a mismatch by any of the usual measures.

"I got a lead that I should write a letter to local attorney John Hay, who sat on the board of a medical research foundation, the Mathers Charitable Foundation," Rod says. "They didn't fund arts programs. I wrote a two-page letter anyway, and six months went by." At the end of 1982, the company's finances were desperate. "I said, 'I need a sign, I need to know that this is what I'm supposed to be doing.' Within a day of that I got a call from John Hay saying, 'Hello, I have a check for you.'"

Though the Mathers Foundation had no history of funding arts organization, it renewed Access Theatre's funding every year. Executive

Director James Handelman, Jr. asked only for a simple letter from Rod each year in order to donate between $10,000 and $50,000 – cornerstone funds for the company.

"Among many other things, they grandfathered *Storm Reading* over the years," Rod says. "But they were an East Coast foundation and most of the board never saw our work." Rod kept in touch, sending reviews, letters from fans, and photographs. "They knew how their money was spent and how many people they affected. We always maintained that human level of interaction with our donors. You can't just operate on your own little island, you have to acknowledge and include people so they know that what they are giving is important, and they can see their investment paying off."

Rod soon learned that not all money was created equal. Many donors were not only specific about the kinds of organizations they supported, but exactly how support could be used. The Santa Barbara Foundation, for example, a longtime Access supporter, exclusively funded capital investments and so helped Access Theatre buy office, sound and video equipment. The Blanche and Irving Laurie Foundation funded the East Coast tour of

Storm Reading. Occasionally, a foundation would specifically invite Rod to apply for a grant. This was the case when the E.L. Weigand Foundation encouraged Rod to request funds for a desperately needed van. An even more unusual example: the Weingart Foundation responded to a request for $7500 with a $10,000 donation to fund youth programs.

"The hardest grants to get are general operating grants because everybody prefers to fund a specific project," Rod says. "There were times over the years where there was an ironic juxtaposition of funds, where we urgently needed operating funds, but we had plenty of project funds. The crunch time was late fall, a typically low time for grants. We might barely be meeting payroll, but have $10,000 in the bank for another program. But you can't spend funds inappropriately, you have to keep them separate and clean. During those times, $1500 or $1000 of unrestricted funds might come in unexpectedly and it was like gold."

"It can also be frustrating because some foundations and government programs only want you to ask for money for new programs," Rod adds. "They ask 'what are you going to develop that's new?' I wanted to say

Kenny and Julia Loggins, advisory board member Jelinda
DeVorzon and Rod, at the benefit premiere of *Disclosure*, 1994.

Access Theatre presented benefit premieres for *Romancing the
Stone*, *Jewel of the Nile*, *War of the Roses*, *Falling Down* and
Disclosure. This was possible through the generosity of Michael
Douglas, Warner Bros, Twentieth Century Fox, and Bruce Corwin
of the Metropolitan Theatres Corporation, and through the
efforts of Jelinda and local volunteers and sponsors.

'Don't ask me to do something new, help our proven programs stay alive.'"

——

One thing grant makers look for is collaboration among organizations, and programs that build community by bringing groups together. In 1985, Access Theatre's *Olly Olly Oxen Free*, an original play about substance abuse and teenagers, toured schools as a collaboration with the National Council on Alcoholism of Santa Barbara. It attracted funds from the State of California Health and Welfare Agency, Department of Alcohol and Drug Programs, and the Santa Barbara County Alcohol Program.

Silent Quake, a video tape about earthquake preparedness for deaf citizens, was funded by the Ventura County Office of Emergency Services. School performances and teachers' guides for the conservation-themed musical *Legend of the Crystal Waters* were supported by the local water districts, and City of Santa Barbara Department of Public Works.

Access Theatre also joined forces with other arts organizations – a sometimes difficult but rewarding way to make art. In 1984, *Kites* was produced with the Valerie Huston Dance

Theatre. The 1985 *Children of a Lesser God* was a co-production with Santa Barbara Repertory Theatre. In 1990, *The Boys Next Door* inaugurated the Center Stage Theater in Santa Barbara, and the company produced eight more shows at the theater.

Flavia and the Dream Maker was produced in cooperation with painter and writer Flavia Weedn. The company collaborated with the Santa Barbara City College Theatre Group to present the Youth Access for the Arts production of *Godspell*, and with Santa Barbara City Schools for *Leap!* These alliances were powerful and imperfect. Financial disputes dampened some of the behind-the-scenes spirit of *Kites*; accessibility issues were sometimes misunderstood by collaborators, and artistic differences had to be resolved.

As Access Theatre grew, Rod and the company helped other organizations, giving a home to the National Association for Theatre and Accessibility. Rod became active as a County Arts Commissioner, and sat on the board of both the Lobero and Center Stage theaters. Access Theatre helped raise funds for other causes through benefit performances. "Our local involvement gives the foundations a bigger return on their investment," Rod explains. "When a patron sees that the community is there for you and rallies to your cause, and you are in turn giving back, they know they are supporting more than just a theater company."

———

The first Access Theatre advisory board was formed in 1982. It was an informal board because the company was not yet incorporated as a non-profit organization. This first board was typical of the kind of grass roots support the company attracted at that time. *Stage Struck*, mounted in that year, had received one of the greatest outpourings of volunteer and in-kind support the company had ever seen. The new, enthusiastic board picked up on this spirit and was instrumental in setting up a tour to Palm Springs for the entire company.

This tour in turn introduced the company to Barbara Sinatra and through her to the Princess Grace Foundation USA, one of Access Theatre's most important early grants. This chain of events exemplifies one of the most important roles of non-profit boards – networking – a process that would bring Access Theatre some of its most important funding.

When Access Theatre incorporated in 1988, a formal board was formed, supported with advisory and honorary boards of community leaders and celebrities. Among the first board members were Rod's father and sister, and playwright Ellen Anderson, whose husband Tom Buhl had been donating typesetting to the company for nearly a decade.

Over the years, the diversity of the board created a lively exchange of ideas. The combination of conservative and liberal viewpoints insured fiscal stability, while enabling the organization to take calculated risks to expand. From the earliest days, board members used their connections to bring in crucial funding and support. Board member Michael Reichert, whose GEM Group of radio and TV stations had given thousands of dollars of advertising, introduced Rod to Dr. Joseph Pollock, who secured funding to pay for the Info Sign open captioning system. Board members Peter de Palma and Michael Douglas introduced the Robert Wood Johnson Jr. Foundation to the company. Peter Seaman brought in *Forrest Gump* creator Bob Zemeckis as an honorary board member.

Board-organized fundraising events ranged from rummage sales to elegant celebrity dinners, and included gala benefit premieres for five of Michael Douglas' films.

One of the chief organizers was Jelinda DeVorzon, a talented hostess who became Rod's friend and cheerleader. Starting in 1982, Jelinda and her husband, composer Barry DeVorzon, donated personally to the company. But just as valuable, the DeVorzons, introduced Access Theatre to their friends in Montecito society, hosting and helping to organize an array of events from celebrity dinners to the premiere parties.

These galas, which attracted up to 2000 guests, were attended by Michael Douglas, and other celebrities including Danny DeVito, Robert Mitchum, Kathleen Turner, Melissa Manchester, James Brolin, and Kate Mulgrew. The events were the ultimate opportunity for in-kind donations. Bianchi Motor Works donated antique cars to carry guests to the curb where they walked up a donated red carpet into the theater, donated by Metropolitan Theatres Corporation. Longtime supporter the Santa Barbara Biltmore Hotel, and local restaurants, catered the receptions. The festivities succeeded through the efforts of dozens of volunteers, especially Jelinda, a gracious but firm practitioner of Southern hospitality, who insured that influential people and potential donors saw Access Theatre in action.

"It was not always comfortable for my friends to see the company," Jelinda recalls, "*Storm Reading* especially was a real eye opener for me and many of my friends. It always seemed a little bit of a risk to involve people, to say 'trust me you really must see this,' but it was always an awakening and people were always moved. It's important to have a strong board to work behind you, to fundraise and use their connections. I'm confident about doing it and I do it with great joy. I see some movement in this country toward accessibility, and it's nice to think that maybe I played a little, tiny part."

—·—

Storm Reading was the most financially productive show in Access Theatre's history. During the peak years of its tour – 1989 through 1994 – revenue accounted for up to 34% of the company's budget, an unusually high percentage for a non-profit arts organization. It was a time of expansion for the company. The incorporation in 1988, the success of *Storm Reading*, and the board of directors opened new possibilities, but also new demands and responsibilities.

HSH Princess Stephanie and HSH Prince Albert of Monaco present Rod Lathim with

the Princess Grace Foundation USA Award, Beverly Hills, 1985.

In 1990, the Access Theatre offices were still a back room in Rod's house, the overflow spilling into his dining room and his garage. The board, specifically president Stan Fishman and Rod's father and sister, started looking for a facility. "On any board there are people who push you past your comfort level and get you to take risks – Stan was that person for Rod," remembers sister Kim Lippincott. Even so, the move into the new offices was traumatic for the grassroots-minded Rod, who had built the company pinching pennies until they squeaked.

By now, it was clear that the organization had to hire staff if it was going to support the success of the company. Thom Rollerson came to his job interview when the company office was still at Rod's house. It was a culture shock for the successful Los Angeles casting agent and salesman. Thom joined the staff anyway as company manager after seeing *Storm Reading* on stage. Over the next five years, he marketed the company aggressively, managed the increasingly successful *Storm Reading* tour and formed a talent bank for actors with disabilities. "I had never really been proud of the tools I had developed in the corporate world," Thom says, "so I was thrilled to be using them for something

meaningful. I thought the sky was the limit. But I got a shock of reality. There are 800 non-profits, just in Santa Barbara." In 1990, a grant from The James Irvine Foundation brought the first director of development Tom Gaffney on board to give the company its first full-time fundraiser.

By the time *The Boys Next Door* opened in 1990, the company budget for shows, education programs, and administration had reached $250,000 and the staff grew to include controller Stuart Eiseman, bookkeeper Jane Park, and office assistant Billie Burke Perkins. Another grant from the Irvine Foundation brought Director of Programs and Community Access Daniel Girard on board in 1994.

In 1992, Harvard Business School graduate Melissa Marsted joined the staff as the new director of development. Marsted soon created new contacts, and brought the company to a new level of funding success. She also helped Access Theatre to pursue more national funding, including grants from the Hearst Foundation and The National Endowment for the Arts.

From the early days, Access Theatre attracted city, county, and state government funds. Director of the Santa Barbara County

Access company members Remi Sandri, Lori
Hennessey, Peter Robertson, Rod and Michael Hughs
accept the 1987 Media Access Award for Outstanding
Contribution by a Corporation or Organization, with
fellow honoree, actress Marlee Matlin.

Arts Commission Patrick Davis says the company was a "rare, model program," impressive for its combination of innovative programs and fiscal conservatism, featuring careful budgets, no debt, and a portfolio full of low-risk Treasury bills.

"When we are allocating our funds, we evaluate for quality, professionalism, fiscal accountability, and the impact of the grant request on the organization's development," Davis says. "They always got the highest score in the county, and were funded at our highest level. This was an achievement, because Rod usually had to convince the panel that a proposed project would develop the organization. We usually prefer to fund things like administrative salaries because they are very easy to account for – the body is in the chair. But we had confidence that when Access Theatre presented us with a project budget it was realistic and would really happen."

The NEA application was difficult for far more bureaucratic reasons – requiring audited books and the proverbial mountain of paperwork, nearly a full-time job for Melissa. In 1993 the NEA turned down Access Theatre, as they often do with first-year applicants; they funded the company in the subsequent three years awarding annual grants ranging from $7500 to $13,500.

"There is no prescription" Melissa says, "I just make sure I never hear 'no' from a funder, but always 'maybe next time.' I rarely take no as final. I reapply, I keep them up to date, and I just keep asking."

Throughout its history, much of Access Theatre's important support came from the generosity of a few key individuals – people who were introduced to the company through personal contacts and fundraising letters, or who sought the company out for themselves. These funds allowed Access Theatre to not only survive but to push into risky areas and to grow. The most dramatic example is the Access Theatre endowment campaign, initiated by a longtime donor with a matching grant in 1993. Based on this gift, the board set a goal for a $1 million principal, which was to remain in the bank untouched in perpetuity to generate annual interest income – a base for each year's fundraising efforts. Those who initiated and contributed to the endowment campaign knew that an endowment, though unusual for a company of Access Theatre's size, was the only way to protect it from the annual struggle for funds. It seemed a new level of financial security might be within reach.

Maxwell House president Chuck Phillips *(left)* presents Rod
(with grandfather David Manwill) with one of Maxwell House's
100 Real Hero Awards, Nashville, 1992. Rod also received
the Santa Barbara School District Alumni of the Year award
for 1989, one of United Cerbral Palsy's Humanitarian Awards
for 1990, and the 1995 *Santa Barbara Magazine* Big Canvas
Award for creative community spirit.

(above) Estelle Getty, advisory board member, Chris Rennolds, Rod and company manager Thom Rollerson, 10th Anniversary Gala reception.

(at left) Rod, Ed Waterstreet, Linda Bove, and guest host Melissa Manchester.

In 1990 Veteran Access Theatre performers and crew from the first ten years gathered at the Lobero Theatre to celebrate the anniversary gala "A Night to Remember" with hosts including Anthony Edwards, Estelle Getty, Melissa Manchester, Kate Mulgrew (at right) and John Randolph.

Kirk and Michael Douglas, *Falling Down*
benefit premiere, Arlington Theater, 1993.

The idea to fund Access Theatre's 1996 production, *Flight* seemed do-able: Michael Douglas offered to appear in a television commercial and donate part of his fee. Douglas' agents were convinced somebody would jump at the chance to have him as spokesperson, and actively sought a match. But there were ultimately no takers willing to abide by Douglas' terms of a subtle product inclusion in a commercial featuring Access Theatre. When it seemed clear the plan would not work, production on *Flight* was halted. The news shook the company to the core.

For the first time in Access Theatre's history there was no way to squeak by, no last minute angel, not enough money to save the show. Rod could not borrow. Nor could he accept drastically reducing the scope of the show, which was supposed to be the jewel of the Cultural Paralympiad, directly following the Atlanta Olympic Games. After a year of development and seven weeks of rehearsal, the cast, crew, and production staff were laid off. *Storm Reading* went to the Cultural Paralympic Festival in place of *Flight* at the invitation of Special Audiences Inc., which used their own grant money to fund the trip.

Ironically, the Access Theatre Endowment Fund was well on its way to its goal, but the accumulating principal was legally bound to the endowment; it could not be touched. Though the future development of the company was looking better than ever, there was not enough money to fund the present – to pay for the show at hand.

"*Flight* was the first time I went into production without all the money in hand, and it was a devastating lesson," Rod says. "It's ironic that after being so careful for all those years, after all the lessons we learned, we took our biggest risk and couldn't pull it off. I let my eyes get too big, and I was reassured by a plan that sounded good. I listened to other people. I listened to my head. I didn't listen to my gut. Money never comes easy – don't ever be fooled into thinking it will – and always, *always* listen to your gut."

The ultimate volunteers and guardian angels, Rod's parents
Kathy and Reg Lathim, at the *War of the Roses* benefit
premiere, Arlington Theatre, Santa Barbara, 1989. "If I didn't
have a very strong foundation of family and support and
knowing I was loved, I couldn't have been free to explore,
and to develop confidence in other people," Rod says. "It
continues to be true; I'm loved, and that was there
underneath whatever Access Theatre accomplished."

"There's something mystical about it, not in a way out sense, but in a very real sense. I remember reading that a mystic is simply one who recognizes a divine child within and lets it out to play in the universe. And I think Rod Lathim has a divine child in him that finds that child in others and invites them out to play in the universe."

Maryellen Kelley, *educator*

"He has this huge knowledge of what humans want, need, desire. He has a sense of what to do when. He's awake."

Ellen K. Anderson, *playwright*

Between 1979 and 1996, as Access Theatre blazed a trail for accessibility in theater and in life, the country began to catch on, passing the Americans With Disabilities Act (ADA) in 1990. At that time, Rod had been creating accessible theater for eleven years, through thirteen original productions.

He had patiently repeated over and over the lessons that seemed self-evident – a human being is a human being; we are all a little disabled; differences can be accommodated. He explained to theater managers that accessible toilets meant nothing if the bathroom was up a flight of steps. He explained to reporters that playwright Neil Marcus was perfectly capable of understanding their questions and answering for himself, that his dystonia had affected his body not his brain. He told actors that, yes, because it was accessible theater there would be a sign language interpreter on stage, and no, it wouldn't ruin their performance.

Rod and company chipped away at assumptions one at a time, and gradually a circle of accessibility widened around Access Theatre. In talkback sessions with audiences after the performances, people spoke of similar revelations again and again, and it always felt good. The company files filled up with gushing, remarkable letters. That felt good too. But after eighteen years, Rod also felt like it was time for people to get the message of equal access and start building on it. He was increasingly uncomfortable as an advocate for people with disabilities, who were now more often speaking up eloquently for themselves.

Whether the world had caught up or not, Rod's personal mission had to expand into the next manifestation.

Rod started acting when he was a child, pressing his sister Kim into service for epic, hours-long puppet shows on a cardboard stage. When Rod landed his first line in the Santa Barbara Junior High School production of *The Wizard of Oz*, he learned the entire script; his parents would sit and listen to him perform it almost nightly in his sleep.

In high school he began volunteering – as president of the Kiwanis-sponsored Key Club and as a counselor and aide for the Muscular Dystrophy Association. He joined Santa Barbara High's A Capella Choir and Madrigal Singers under director Phyllis Zimmerman. Her legendary policies of discipline and artistic excellence instilled her students with a work ethic and sense of possibility that many have never forgotten.

"I had true spiritual experiences singing," Rod says, "When you are singing as an ensemble, there is a unity, an energy that you can't deny, and that makes you stand at attention and be very present. It becomes a common bond among people, and the memory sticks with people even after they are no longer singing together. Through that experience, I knew in a very real way that there was a link among the arts, spirituality and communication."

But Rod realized that the inspiring opportunities he was having in the arts were completely unavailable to people he was getting to know through the Muscular Dystrophy Association and in his personal life. He decided to seek out a career for himself that might help close this gap.

After high school Rod left for the University of Kansas to pursue a degree in music therapy. But his humanistic, spiritual ideas were out of place in what seemed to him an impersonal, behaviorist program. One day, playing guitar absentmindedly in his dorm room, he had a kind of epiphany. He was sure he had glimpsed his future, though only in the most shadowy of forms. Soon after, Rod left his studies, came home to Santa Barbara and started on his path to Access Theatre.

At the time, the ADA was eleven years away. There was no model for what Rod wanted to do, except his sense that inclusion was a valid mission, and that art was a way for people to grow, to express themselves and come together. Just as importantly, Rod had artistic ambitions – he wanted to write and produce original work. Access Theatre was not a service organization and an accessible *Oklahoma* just wasn't the point. So Rod's personal artistic goals had everything to do with how the company matured, the work they did and the message they put forth.

Even as Access Theatre grew to attract substantial funding from major sources, Rod was a reluctant administrator. He threw all his energy behind it, but only because he had to, in order to move on to the rehearsals, the performances, and the tours – the things he really thrived on. As the years passed, though the company hired talented people to help him, though the boards supported him fervently, the burden of being in charge of an organization, and being responsible for its survival, became heavier. One donor in particular recognized this, and initiated the Access Theatre endowment fund. If the endowment campaign succeeded, the constant pressure to raise funds and meet donors guidelines would be eased. It seemed for a time that Rod could expand his artistic vision with Access Theatre, and try new and challenging works of art.

When Rod began work on *Flight*, it was to fulfill an artistic idea he had been dreaming about for years. He envisioned a musical performance piece inspired by Cirque du Soleil, full of abstract choreography that would completely blur the distinctions among cast members with and without disabilities. He spent months casting a multi-talented group of artists who could sing, dance, and improvise. Composers Mark Henderson and Greg Kuhn went to work on lush melodies, while the cast began working with the theatrical flying apparatus, experimenting with flying pas de deux and flying comedy, even flying in a wheelchair. Just as *Flight* was shaping up to be one of Access Theatre's best artistic efforts, it floundered on a lack of funding and came to a painful and discouraging end.

But *Flight*'s demise also clarified something for Rod. His personal direction lay away from Access Theatre as he had known it. Rod did not want to be an administrator anymore; he didn't want to lead, he wanted to create. He also wanted to give himself time to pursue a relationship, a part of his life which had been unexplored in the years he devoted to Access Theatre.

Rod decided to leave the company. The volunteer board of directors spent two difficult months evaluating what to do: whether to keep the company open, whether the mission was still clear, whether to search for a new artistic director and director of development and reinvent Access Theatre. Ultimately, the board decided to close the company, and Rod locked the doors himself on November 31, 1996.

— . —

So what is Access Theatre's legacy? On a practical level, the Access Theatre Endowment continues, administered by the Santa Barbara Foundation to support accessible theater projects. The Young Playwrights Festival and other youth programs continue at Santa Barbara's Center Stage Theater under the direction of Daniel Girard and Lily Wong. Center Stage also took over the company's audience accessibility equipment to make it available to any local theater production free of charge. But what of the bigger picture – all the performances, artists, audiences, and achievements that added up over the years?

"As I look back over it, it's hard for me to focus on the details," Rod says. "At its most basic, I think Access Theatre was a framework for a life process. It was a place where lives converged. When people interacted, they embellished each other, and sometimes they didn't – that's just like life – and we succeeded together, and sometimes we didn't. But all the intersections were important – the good, the

bad, the frustrating, the affirming – because it was a coming together of human lives – a lot of lives.

"That's something I take away with me. Because once you have experienced it, you want more – that coming together of lives and the power it has. One of the fears I have now is that as a society we'll move farther away from being human and valuing face to face, eye to eye contact and communication. We don't get a lot of opportunity to look each other in the eyes and see who we really are – that we're more than just physical bodies, that there is something to us that is special, unique, and worth nurturing. So I'm motivated to continue to create original theater that promotes people to people contact. I come away from Access Theatre with a feeling of peace and completion and an absolute certainty that this kind of living theater can make a difference in the world.

"I know that many people feel jaded, they don't want happy endings, they don't want to be touched, they don't want to be human anymore. They embrace violence and inhumane values as the norm. I'm not going to buy into that. There have always been people who classify Access as the warm fuzzy theater, and I used to resent that, and I don't anymore. Because there's value in doing things that touch us on a real honest human level. And happy endings are not bad. We need *more* happy endings. I'm in *favor* of happy endings."

Cliff Austin, *Footlight Fantasy*, Lobero Theatre, 1981

repertory

Circus of Life

Written/Directed by Rod Lathim

Assistant director: Darcy Fluitt

Accompanist: Jenean Johnson

Choreography by Mory Alvarez, Darcy Fluitt, Pamela Easterday, Rod Lathim and Stacy Sutley

Premiered May 10, 1979, Lobero Theatre, Santa Barbara, California with the following cast: Cathy Acton, Sheila Altman, Tiffany Bailey, Dina Baker, Jack Ball, Sonia Bermudez, Renee Blakeslee, Becky Blue, Libby Booth, Norman Dahl, Greg De Silva, Leslie Donovan, Donna Entz, Noah Erenberg, Danny Fisher, Darcy Fluitt, Harry Gilman, Jonathan Goddard, Susan Goodnight, Phillip Greig, Robert Hammerstrom, Edward Huff, Caroline Hunter, Andy Isaacs, Davis Isabell, Peter Jacobs, Andy Kaufman, Patty Kellogg, Betsy Kenner, Merril Krassner, Jill Ladin, Sue Lang, Sherrie Leaver, Robin Lincke, Cathy Lodge, Rosana McCullough, Shelly Michaud, Markley Mogan, Lynn Mondschein, Sivea Moore, Katie Mudd, Dede Nickols, David Norcross, Allison Paradise, Bobby Perry, Willie Ponder, Steve Reynolds, Tammy Roth, Missy Runnels, Teresa Shaefer, Candy Stoddard, Mary Story, Dennis Subica, Carolyn Sullivan, Stacy Sutley, John Tigerman, Alicia Torres, Hank Underwood, Diana Valle, Barry Verheuff, Teri Wilson and Laura Winter

Through Our Eyes

Written/Directed/Choreographed by Rod Lathim

Music by J. Denny Moore

Art Direction by Susan Warren

Production Coordinator: Paula Emigh

Premiered May 1, 1980, Lobero Theatre, Santa Barbara, California with the following cast: Cathy Acton, Tiffany Bailey, Marilyn Bakken, Jack Ball, Renee Blakeslee, Libby Booth, Patty Burnquist, Rosemarie Carrao, Peter Cooney, Norman Dahl, Jeanne Daze, Leslie Donovan, Noah Erenberg, Danny Fisher, Garret Garcia, Harry Gilman, Jonathan Goddard, Steven Goranson, Lori Grabowski, Gary Greco, Sherri Habush, Robert Hammerstrom, Kathy Heitzman, Edward Huff, Andy Isaacs, Beverly Jerup, Patty Kellogg, Betsy Kenner, Dina Lacey-Baker, Jill Ladin, Robin Lincke, John Henry Lockie, Cathy Lodge, Markley Mogan, Lynn Mondschein, Sivea Moore, Katie Mudd, Cindy O'Shaughnessy, Allison Paradise, Bobby Perry, Craig Plapinger, Willie Ponder, Greg Raizik, Tammy Roth, Chris Rudy, Missy Runnels, Farhang Salehi, Teresa Shaefer, Susie Soheili, Andrea Srnka, Susie Stanton, Mary Story, Tom Stroble, Dennis Subica, Terry Talley, Alicia Torres, Hank Underwood, Diana Valle, Mary Walker, Mary Lou Whelan, Judson Wilcox, Laura Winter and Tina Wright with members of the Santa Barbara High School A Cappella Choir

Take a Card, Any Card

By Martin Kimeldorf

Directed by Rod Lathim

Music by Mark Colin Henderson and Rod Lathim

Sign Language Interpretation by Pamela Larson and Robaire

Production opened September 17, 1980, Lobero Theatre, Santa Barbara, California with the following cast: Michelle Bennett, Corky Borgmann, Don Cantrell, Paul Davies, Linda Egar, Jeff Gorham, John Goulet, Claire Sears Grammer, Oliver Nelson Hamilton, Andy Jensen, Rod Lathim, Pat Lauer, Juli Lyon, Peter McCorkle, Elizabeth A. McGrath, Alice Parkinson, Theresa Peretik, Craig Plapinger, Mary Gaines Read, Rose Anna Vitetta, Virginia Zavalishin and Walter Zeni

Footlight Fantasy

Written/Directed by Rod Lathim and Michael Hughs

Original Music by Mark Colin Henderson

Choreography by Betty Simmons, Michael Hughs, Rod Lathim
and Beverly Latimer

Sign Language Interpretation by Francine Buker and Rod Lathim

Premiered April 30, 1981, Lobero Theatre, Santa Barbara, California with
the following cast: Cliff Austin, Newton Bass, Ron Berry, Francine Buker,
Rosemarie Carrao, Noelle Clearwater, Jeanne Daze, Gina Dyson, Bruce
Gilchrist, Lori Grabowski, Fran Grobben, Lori Hennessey, Mark Janisch,
Patty Kellogg, Rod Lathim, Cathy Lodge, Theresa Peretik, Craig Plapinger,
Craig Renn, Marty Ross, Betty Simmons, Michael Spencer, Dennis Subica
and Paula Tevis

Signing Off

Directed by Rod Lathim and Susan Warren

Original Music by Mark Colin Henderson

Sign Language Interpretation by Francine Buker and Peter M. Robertson

Premiered November 15, 1981 Victoria Street Theatre, Santa Barbara,
California; performed through 1981 with the following cast: Suzy
Beckman, Francine Buker, Julie Chirman, Susanne Douthit, Lori
Hennessey, Peter McCaffrey, Peter McCorkle, Anna Marie Medina,
Solomon Smaniotto and Evilio (Victor) Torres

Stage Struck

Written by Rod Lathim, Susan Warren and Peter McCorkle

with additional material by Larry Davis and Marty Ross

Directed by Rod Lathim

Music by Mark Colin Henderson

Lyrics by Connie Samovitz

Additional Music/Lyrics by Shelley Rink and Marty Ross

Musical Director and Conductor: Shelley Rink

Choreography by Mike Downey and Peter McCorkle

Scenic Design by Rod Lathim, Joe Hennessey, Craig Wcislo,

Susan Warren and Juliana Terada

Lighting Design by Maryi Sagady and Jerry Griffin

Sign Language Interpretation by Francine Buker and Peter M. Robertson

Premiered May 13, 1982, Lobero Theatre, Santa Barbara, California;
performed through 1983 with the following cast: Dana Adams, Suzy
Beckman, Francine Buker, Kathleen Corby, Larry Davis, Stephen Day,
Stephen Fountain, Lynn Gallagher, Mitch Galper, Fran Grobben, Oliver
Hamilton, Lori Hayward, Lori Hennessey, Kathleen Henry, Kristin
Hollern, Craig Hyams, Mark Janisch, Linda Kaplan, Rob Looker, Peter
McCaffrey, Peter McCorkle, Anna Marie Medina, Bret Nighman, Valerie
Oesterling, Theresa Peretik, Lea Perrizo, Karen Rink, Peter M. Robertson,
Florence Ross, Marty Ross, Karen Ruhl, Remi Sandri, Jay Shobe, Betty
Simmons, Richard Sirois, Kathy Spang, Sabrina Springer, Dennis Subica,
Juliana Terada, Evilio (Victor) Torres, Rose Anna Vitetta, Kathryn Voice,
Mishel Walden, Jake Weber and Craig Wcislo

Finger Talk

Directed by Rod Lathim

Choreography by Peter McCorkle

Original Music/Lyrics by Marty Ross, Mark Colin Henderson,
Rod Lathim, Peter McCorkle and Katie Voice

Sign Language Interpretation by Francine Buker, Peter M. Robertson and
Evilio (Victor) Torres

Premiered October, 1982, Garvin Theatre, Santa Barbara, California;
performed through 1984 with the following cast: Bo Ayer, Francine Buker,
Matthew Mark Campos, Lori Hennessey, Kathleen Henry, Peter
McCaffrey, Peter McCorkle, Anna Marie Medina, Peter M. Robertson,
Solomon Smaniotto, Evilio (Victor) Torres and Kathryn Voice

Kites

Conceived/staged by Valerie Huston, Rod Lathim and Peter McCorkle

Music by Mark Colin Henderson

Lyrics by Eddie Glickman

Musical Director and Conductor: Shelley Rink

Scenic Design by L.K. Strasburg

Lighting Design by Jennifer Norris

Sign Language Interpretation by Francine Buker and Peter M. Robertson

Premiered October 25, 1984, Lobero Theatre, Santa Barbara, California; performed through 1985 with the following cast: Francine Buker, Gina De Angelo, Robin Ferry, Robin Fortyune, John Gaydos, Leslie Johnson, Evelyn Kobayashi, Rod Lathim, Greg Lara, Cathy Lazarus, Peter McCorkle, William Ramsdell, Pat Ramsey, Diane Reddy, Peter M. Robertson, Solomon Smaniotto, Evilio (Victor) Torres and Kathryn Voice

Children of a Lesser God

By Mark Medoff

Co-produced by Access Theatre and Santa Barbara Repertory Theatre

Directed by Rod Lathim

Scenic Design by Theodore Michael Dolas

Lighting Design by Gerard Griffin

Costume Design by Joan Mather

Sign Language Interpretation by Fran Buker and Peter M. Robertson

Production opened July 5, 1985, Garvin Theatre, Santa Barbara, California with the following cast: Francine Buker, Tod Fortner, Amy Jackson, Ian Edward Kelly, Remi Sandri, Bobbie Beth Scoggins, Candice Taylor and Marnee Wafer

Olly Olly Oxen Free

Written by Davida Wills

Directed by Rod Lathim

Music by Mark Colin Henderson

Lyrics by Eddie Glickman

Choreography by Peter McCorkle

Lighting Design by Michael Johnson

Sign Language Interpretation by Francine Buker and Peter M. Robertson

Premiered February, 1985, Lobero Theatre, Santa Barbara, California and toured through 1985 with the following cast: Ann Bengry, Mary Ann Bleier, Steve Ferguson, Stephen Kay, Joi Martins, Tiffany Renee, Russell Ricard, Tracy Silver, Brian Sullivan and Marnee Wafer

Legend of the Crystal Waters

Written by Doug Haverty

Directed by Rod Lathim

Music by Mark Colin Henderson

Lyrics by David M. Strauss

Choreography by Peter McCorkle and Rod Lathim

Scenic Design by Erica Zaffarano

Lighting Design by Patricia L. Frank

Costume Design by Pamela Shaw

Sign Language Interpretation by Francine Buker and Peter M. Robertson

Premiered February 28, 1987, Lobero Theatre, Santa Barbara, California with the following cast: Robert Ayer, Francine Buker, Lori Hennessey, Daniel Hiatt, Ian Edward Kelly, David McKay, Peter M. Robertson, Tal Sanders, Remi Sandri, Greg Schultz, Tamara Turner, Kathryn Voice and voices of David Hopson, Kim Insley, Kenny Loggins and Rosalyn Sistrom

Storm Reading

Written by Roger Marcus, Neil Marcus and Rod Lathim

Based on the writings of Neil Marcus

Additional material by Matthew Ingersoll and Kathryn Voice

Directed by Rod Lathim

Original Music by Mark Colin Henderson, Gregory Kuhn, Barbara Hirsch and Ilana Eden

Scenic Design by Jonathan Sabo/*Touring Set by* Theodore Michael Dolas

Lighting Design by Theodore Michael Dolas

Costume Design by Janis Martin and Janet Doran-Veevers

Sign Language Interpretation by Kathryn Voice

Premiered March 4, 1988, Lobero Theatre, Santa Barbara, California; performed through 1994 with the following cast: Matthew Ingersoll, Neil Marcus, Roger Marcus and Kathryn Voice

The Boys Next Door

By Tom Griffin

Directed by Rod Lathim

Scenic/Lighting Design by Theodore Michael Dolas

Costume Design by Abra Flores

Sign Language Interpretation by Francine Buker and Kathryn Voice

Production opened August 22, 1990, Center Stage Theater, Santa Barbara, California with the following cast: Dirk Blocker, Marc Buckland, Karyl Lynn Burns, Kellie Diamond, Anthony Edwards, Richard Hochberg, Henry Holden, Matthew Ingersoll, Susan Kern, Haven Mitchell and Billie Burke Perkins

At Long Last Leo

By Mark Stein

Directed by Frank Condon

Music by Michael Mortilla

Scenic/Lighting Design by Theodore Michael Dolas

Costume Design by Abra Flores

Sign Language Interpretation by Kathryn Voice

Production opened May 10, 1991 Center Stage Theater, Santa Barbara, California with the following cast: Bonnie Bartlett, Chet Carlin, Tyler Dumm, Rod Lathim, Victoria Ann Lewis, Delta Giordano Morgan and Kathryn Voice

Flavia and the Dream Maker

Written by Doug Haverty, *Based on the book by* Flavia Weedn

Directed by Rod Lathim

Music by Shelly Markham

Lyrics by Bob Garrett

Choreography by Dan Mojica

Scenic Design by Alison Yerxa

Lighting Design by Theodore Michael Dolas

Costume Design by Abra Flores

Sign Language Interpretation by Michael Purcell

Premiered November 8, 1991, Center Stage Theater, Santa Barbara, California with the following cast: Noah Gaines, Anne Jacoby, C.J. Jones, Patty Neumeyer, Michael Purcell, Fran Ripplinger and Clarke Thorell

Listen for Wings!

Written by Ellen K. Anderson

Directed by Jenny Sullivan

Scenic Design by Mica

Lighting Design by Nathan Stein

Costume Design by Clifford Olson

Sign Language Interpretation by Kathryn Voice

Premiered May 15, 1992, Center Stage Theater, Santa Barbara, California; performed through 1992 with the following cast: John Fink, Cheryl Herrington, Val Limar, Rod Lathim, Billie Burke Perkins, Kathryn Voice and voice of Thomas W. Rollerson

The Living Cartoon

By C.J. Jones

Performed by C.J. Jones, January 23, 1993, Center Stage Theater, Santa Barbara, California and toured through 1995

In-Sight

Written by Ty Granaroli with Nadja Forest and Rod Lathim

Directed by Rod Lathim and Nadja Forest

Music by Mark Colin Henderson and Gregory Kuhn

Sign Language Interpretation by Francine Buker and Michael Purcell

Premiered May 14, 1993, Center Stage Theater, Santa Barbara, California with the following cast: Debbie Daniel, Tyler Dumm, Noah Gaines, Elizabeth Heller, Camille Mills Kitchen and Daniel Seward

Twice Blessed

By Cynthia Lee and Art Metrano

Directed by Rod Lathim

Scenic/Lighting Design by Theodore Michael Dolas

Sign Language Interpretation by Jo Black

Performed by Art Metrano with Jo Black, December 3-19, 1993, Center Stage Theater, Santa Barbara, California

Godspell

Conceived and Originally Directed by John-Michael Tebelak

Music and Lyrics by Stephen Schwartz

Directed/choreographed by Peter McCorkle

Music Director: Pam Herzog

Scenic/Lighting Design by Douglas Tal Sanders

Costume Design by Dairine Davison

Sign Language Interpretation by Michael Purcell

Production opened July 14, 1994, The Studio Theatre, Garvin Theatre Complex, Santa Barbara, California with the following cast: Nicole Danielle Barrett, Jamie Martin-Chamberlin, Noah Leigh Gaines, Quinn Gonzales, Michael Hampton, Joyce Kondak, Aaron Levin, Tori Lewis, Gioia Marchese, Sean Maurer, Heidi Merrick, Judson Pearce Morgan, Sarah Petersen, Michael Purcell, Bill Sweeney and Alysa Rossetti Zeuli

Stix and Stonz

Written by Ty Granaroli

Directed by Rod Lathim and Nadja Forest

Sign Language Interpretation by Michael Purcell

Premiered March, 1994; performed through 1995 with the following cast: David Aumentado, Nicole Danielle Barrett, Ali Burk, Devon Shea Colin, Maria Goena, Eileen Gonzales, Ingrid Holden, Nora Lange, Colton O'Neil, Geren Piltz, Ben Provo, Michael Purcell, Richard Stokes and Josh Welsh

Belle's On Wheels

By Jaehn Clare

Directed by Rod Lathim

Scenic/Lighting Design by Theodore Michael Dolas

Sign Language Interpretation by Michael Purcell

Performed by Jaehn Clare with Billie Burke Perkins and Michael Purcell, January 19-22, 1995 at the Center Stage Theater, Santa Barbara, California

Leap! A Musical Quest

Conceived by Ty Granaroli, Rod Lathim, Nadja Forest and Michael Purcell

Written by Ty Granaroli

Directed by Rod Lathim

Choreography by Michael Purcell, Peter McCorkle and Nadja Forest

Music by Mark Colin Henderson and Gregory Kuhn

Lyrics by Johnny Elkins

Music Director: Pam Herzog

Scenic/Lighting Design by Douglas Tal Sanders

Costume Design by Dairine Davison

Sign Language Interpretation by Michael Purcell

Premiered July 15, 1995, Santa Barbara High School Auditorium, Santa Barbara, California with the following cast: John Carter, Corey Elias, Holly Ferguson, Laurie Gold, Michael Gonzales, Quinn Gonzales, Tobias Jelinek, Megan Lee, Kathleen Le Pley, Betty Mann, Gioia Marchese, Austin McCormick, Tony Miratti, Judson Pearce Morgan, Michael Peacock and Jon Rickman

Flight

Conceived by Rod Lathim, Ty Granaroli, and Michael Purcell

Written by Kenneth Robins

Directed by Rod Lathim

Choreographed by Suzie Sherr

Music by Mark Colin Henderson and Gregory Kuhn

Technical Direction/Scenic Design: Douglas Tal Sanders

Lighting Design: Martyn Bookwalter

Costume Design: Marcos Lutyens

Developed in workshop March through May 1996 with the following cast: Stuart Eiseman, Jeff Horny, Kim Jones, Diana Jordan, Troy Kotsur, Casey Pieretti, Michael Purcell, and Vae

major donors

Government and Service Agencies

City of Santa Barbara Promotional Funds

The Santa Barbara County Arts
   Partnership Program

State of California Area IX Developmental
   Disabilities Board

California Arts Council

National Endowment for the Arts

SB County Schools, Bill Cirone, Superintendent

Santa Barbara City College
   Continuing Education

Santa Barbara Recreation Department

Ventura County Office of Emergency Services

The Santa Barbara County Alcohol Program

Santa Barbara Association for
   Retarded Citizens

National Council on Alcoholism of
   Santa Barbara

California Association for Neurologically
   Handicapped

Neighborhood Arts

Foundations

Amgen Foundation

Arco Foundation

BankAmerica Foundation

Bialis Family Foundation

George V. and Rena G. Castagnola
   Family Foundation

Charles E. Culpeper Foundation

Douglas Charitable Trust

Douglas Charitable Foundation

Flintridge Foundation

Edward T. Foley Foundation

Fund for Santa Barbara

William Randolph Hearst Foundation

James Irvine Foundation

Ann Jackson Family Foundation

John Percival and Mary C. Jefferson
   Endowment Fund

Robert Wood Johnson Jr. Charitable Trust

Mayer/Morris Kaplan Foundation

Joseph P. Kennedy Jr. Foundation

Kingsley Foundation

Achille Levy Foundation

Blanche and Irving Laurie Foundation

La Vista Foundation for the Blind and
   Physically Disabled

The Lobero Theatre Foundation

G. Harold and Leila Y. Mathers
   Charitable Foundation

Richard Harlow Mead Foundation

NEC Foundation of America

New York Times Company Foundation

Pacific Telesis Foundation

Plum Foundation

Dr. Joseph and Helene Pollock Foundation

Princess Grace Foundation USA

Roth Family Foundation

Santa Barbara Foundation

Santa Barbara Jaycees

Jay M. Schechter Philanthropic Fund

Shubert Foundation

Partnership for the Children of Santa
   Barbara County

Phillip Francis Siff Educational Foundation

Harold Simmons Foundation

Snider Foundation

Sidney Stern Memorial Trust

Towbes Foundation

Wallis Foundation

Weingart Foundation

E.L. Wiegand Foundation

Wood-Claeyssens Foundation

Zalk Foundation

Businesses

3M Company

Aidan Bradley Photography

American Express Companies

Art Resources Custom Framing

AT&T Wireless/Cellular One

Bianchi Motor Company

Gerry Brady/Lightweight Structural Designs

Tom Buhl Imaging

Chevron USA

Christensen and Drake

Clarke Design

Come Fly a Kite

Craviotto Ironworks

Creative Artists Agency

Day & Night

Deckers Outdoor Corporation

El Encanto Hotel

Everest & Jennings

Exxon Company, USA

Faces International

First American Title Insurance Company

First Congregational Church

Frontier Communications

Franciscan Inn

The Gem Group

Graham Chevrolet-Geo-Nissan

Gregg Motors

Harry Warren Music Company/
   Four Jays Music Publishing

Incentive Destination Productions

IDS/American Express Financial Services

KCOY TV

KEYT TV/Smith Broadcasting of
   Santa Barbara

KIST Radio

K-LITE/KTMS Radio

KMGQ Radio

Landmark Entertainment Group
Los Angeles Reader
Marketing Innovations International, Inc
Megan Kitchen Graphics
Metropolitan Theatres Corporation
Montecito Bank and Trust
Northern Trust Bank of California
Oakwood Apartments
Palazzio Trattoria
Panasonic Company West
Paradise Café
Pepsi-Cola Company
Phonic Ear
Pitts and Bachmann Realtors
Quantum Video
Sambo's Restaurants
Sanford Winery
Santa Barbara Athletic Club
Santa Barbara Bank and Trust
Santa Barbara Four Seasons Biltmore Hotel
Santa Barbara Independent
Santa Barbara News-Press
Santa Barbara Research GO-CLUB
Santa Barbara Scenic
Santa Barbara Travel Bureau
Sanwa Bank
Smith Hemion Productions
Specialty Photo
Sprecher Design House
State of the Arts
Tropicana Inn
20th Century Fox
UCSB Extension Marketing
Upham Hotel
Warner Bros.
Weedn Design
Wells Fargo Bank

Individuals

Anonymous
Anonymous
Jesse and Nancy Alexander
Rich Ayling
Estate of Margaret Azpell
Ms. Bonnie Bartlett
Jeffrey and Margo Barbakow
Barbara Benziger
Mr. and Mrs. David W. Bermant
Susan Bower
Ken Boxer
Mr. Chapin Burks
John DeLoreto
Victoria DeLoreto
Barry and Jelinda DeVorzon
Theodore Michael Dolas
Michael and Diandra Douglas
Anthony Edwards
Ned Emerson and Ann Lippincott
Jean Feigenbaum
Mr. and Mrs. Robert Martin Fell
Mr. and Mrs. Stanley Fishman
Mr. and Mrs. Harold Frank
Mr. and Mrs. Marshall Geller
Gary Goddard
George Goldberg
Arthur and Laurie Gross-Shaefer
Mr. John Hay
Art and Hazel Hopson
Dave and Karen Hopson
Rhiannon Howell
Virginia Hunter
Kathy Ireland
Palmer Jackson
Susan Jorgensen
In memory of Virginia Kelley

Marty and Karen Kinrose
Vera and Erik Krogh
Mrs. Marion Lamont
Reg and Kathy Lathim
Kim and Bill Lippincott
Kenny Loggins
Jon and Lillian Lovelace
Mr. and Mrs. Eli Luria
Dr. and Mrs. Harris Meisel
Ron Meyer
Mr. and Mrs. Laurence K. Miller
Deborah and Michael McCormick
Kate Mulgrew
Zeta S. Noel
Mr. and Mrs. Roger Oates
Mr. and Mrs. Thomas Pollock
Mrs. C.W. Partridge
Mr. and Mrs. David A. Pitts
Robert Potter
Michael Reichert
Lucille Robinson
Mr. and Mrs. Simon Ross
Mr. and Mrs. Peter Seaman
Carol Servin
Mr. and Mrs. Phil Shipley
Herb and Diane Simon
Scott and Gemina Soule
Margo and Dan Sinclair
Bruce and Lydia Strathdee
Ron Stever
Jenny Sullivan
Sam and Sandra Tyler
John and Barbara Wilson
Robert and Mary Ellen Zemeckis

boards and staff

Thanks to all the dedicated people who have served on the Board of Directors of Access Theatre, Inc., for their vision, endless hours of work and valuable support

Board

Ellen K. Anderson
Robert Ayer
Carl Battles
Jack Bianchi
Shawn Conroy Blom
Nori Burk
Karyl Lynn Burns
Michael Colin
John DeLoreto
Victoria DeLoreto
Peter DePalma
Stan Fishman
Thomas Gaffney
David Hopson
Megan Kitchen
Reg Lathim
Kim Lippincott
Steve Miller
Patty Neumeyer
Michael Reichert
Julie Rodriguez
Peter Seaman
Carol Servin
Sam Tyler

Advisory Board

Nancy Alexander
Fred Allen
William Cirone
Robert Egan
Roberta Fishman
David Fishman
Nikki Allyn Grosso
Hazel Hopson
Rhiannon Howell
Mary Judge
Lisa Kasteler
Kathy Lathim
Neil Marcus
Dr. Harris Meisel
Melody Meisel
Ron Meyer
Billie Burke Perkins
Chris Rennolds
Rosalyn Sistrom
Dr. Bruce Strathdee
Jenny Sullivan
David Wright

Honorary Board

Barry DeVorzon
Jelinda DeVorzon
Michael Douglas
Anthony Edwards
Marshall Geller
Kathy Ireland
Kenny Loggins
Rue McClanahan
Kate Mulgrew
John Randolph
David Seltzer
Mary Ellen Zemeckis
Robert Zemeckis

Administrative Staff

Rod Lathim *Founder/Artistic Director*

Thomas Ward Rollerson *Company Manager*

Melissa Marsted, Thomas Gaffney, Todd Ortone
Development Directors

Daniel Girard *Director of Programs and Community Access*

Peter McCorkle *Youth Theatre Director*

Sue Dumm *Accessibility Services Coordinator*

Stuart Eiseman *Controller*

Kathy Rem, Jane Park,
Bookkeepers

Billie Burke Perkins, Lori Guynes, Francine Buker
Administrative Assistants

acknowledgements

In addition to the many people mentioned in this book, and all who have joined in this journey, I would like to offer my personal thanks to: My entire family for their unending love and support: Reg and Kathy Lathim; Kim and Bill Lippincott; David and Helen Manwill; Mary Ellen Cokeley; Henrietta Emerson and Emily.

And to Ellen K. Anderson; Anthony Askew; Rich Ayling; Abelino Bailon; Mrs. Florence Beard; Gary and Ellen Bialis; Laura Bialis; Aiden Bradley; Mary Jo Buchanan; Tom Buhl; Francine Buker; Donna Chaplin; Bill Cirone; Bruce Corwin; Gwen Coxon; Patrick Davis; Victoria DeLoreto; Peter DePalma; Barry and Jelinda DeVorzon; Ted Dolas; Colleen Dougherty; Michael Douglas; Kirk and Anne Douglas; Anthony Edwards; Stuart Eiseman; Darcy Fluitt; Sue Dumm; Jean Feigenbaum; John and Sharky Fink; Nadja Forest; Thomas Gaffney; Daniel Girard; Ty Granaroli; Nikki Allyn Grosso; Lily Guild; Lori Guynes; James Handelman Jr.; Doug Haverty; John Hay; Shaun Hardin; Mark Henderson; Lori, Anne and Joe Hennessey; Dan Hiatt; Anita Ho; Dave Hopson; Rhiannon Howell; Michael Hughs; Matthew Ingersoll; Nancy Keele; Maryellen Kelley; Martin Kimeldorf; Marty Kinrose; Greg Lee; Aaron Levin; Deborah Lewis; Kenny Loggins; Marjorie Luke; Neil Marcus; Melissa Marsted; Nancy Martin; Peter McCorkle; Melody Meisel; Harriet Miller; Dr. Harris and Fredda Meisel; Nancy Moore; Kate Mulgrew; Susi Murray; Terry Nelson; Dann Netter; Lupe Olvera; Pamala Oslie; Jane Park; Ed Parker; Billie Burke Perkins; Robert Potter; Michael Purcell; Greg Pullis; Harold Reeves; Shelley Rink; Thomas Ward Rollerson; Brooke Rye; Wayne Sabbak; Connie Samovitz, Tal Sanders; Remi Sandri; Clark Sayre; David Schenkel; Michael D. Schley; Devin Scott; Dr. William Sears; Gary Smith; Karen Spotten; Katherine Stackpoole; Margaret Staton; Mary Staton; Jenny Sullivan; Clarke Thorell; Sister Trinitas; Katie Voice; Cynthia Wisehart; Erica Zaffarano; Phyllis Zimmerman,

...and all the actors, designers, musicians, writers, staff and crew, with whom I had the pleasure of collaborating,

...and the audiences with whom we have shared our work.

Rod Lathim, December, 1996

photo credits

The following photographers
generously contributed their
work to this book.

Cover
Jeff Brouws

Back Cover
Michael Hughs

Beginnings

Jonathan Fletcher
(pp. 14, 27 bottom, 29)

David E. Schenkel
(pp. 19, 21, 23)

Len Wood / Santa Barbara
News-Press
(pp. 30, 31, 33)

Wayne Kjar
(pp. 17, 20)

Jurgen Hilmer
(p. 27 top)

Michael Hughs
(p. 25)

Steven:
Stage Struck

Deborah Hollern
(pp. 45, 48, 51)

Michael Hughs
(pp. 37, 47 top)

Randy Hopson
(p. 43)

Jesse Alexander
(p. 44)

Lori: Speaking
from the Heart

Michael Hughs

On Sign Language
Interpretation

Christopher Vore
(pp. 67, 71)

Michael Hughs
(pp. 76 right, 77)

Patricia Roberts
(p. 73)

Rod Lathim
(p. 81)

Courtesy Santa Barbara
News-Press
(p. 75)

Robin and Leslie:
Pas de Deux

Michael Hughs
*(pp. 82, 85, 87 bottom, 88 top,
89, 106)*

Cara Moore
(pp. 88 bottom, 91, 93)

Jesse Alexander
(p. 87 top)

Tamara:
A Mermaid's Tale

Michael Hughs
(pp. 99, 101, 105 top, 109)

Scott Harrison/Ventura
County Star
(pp. 94, 97)

Rod Lathim
(p. 100)

Jay Thompson
(p. 107 right)

Neil: The Storm

Richard A. Carter
(pp. 113, 119, 121, 123 bottom)

Rod Lathim
(pp. 117, 123 top, 127, 131)

Christopher Gardner
(pp. 110, 118)

Susan Jorgensen
(p. 125)

On Stagecraft and
Accessibility

Rod Lathim
*(pp. 144 bottom, 144 center, 145,
149)*

Christopher Vore
(pp. 138, 139, 143)

Michael Hughs
(pp. 135, 144 top)

Remi, Susan
and Leo:
Three Plays

Michael Hughs
(pp. 154, 155, 159)

Christopher Gardner
(pp. 161, 163, 165)

Christopher Vore
(pp. 167, 170, 171)

Rod Lathim
(pp. 169, 156, 164)

Anne and Clarke:
The Dream
Makers

Christopher Vore

Billie: Winging It

Christopher Vore

Jud, Tyler, Devon
and David: A New
Generation

Rod Lathim
(pp. 198, 201, 203 right, 211)

Steve Malone
(pp. 213, 215)

P.J. Heller
(p. 203 left)

Michael Hughs
(p. 205)

Rock Dumm
(p. 207 left)

Daniel Girard
(p. 207 bottom)

On Funding and
Support

Richard A. Carter /
Santa Barbara News-Press
(p. 223, 232 center, 232 bottom)

Michael Hughs
(p. 219)

Alan Berliner
(p. 227)

Christopher Vore
(p. 232 top)

Christopher Gardner
(p. 233)

Charles Stock
(p. 235)

Courtesy Media Access
(p. 229)

Courtesy Maxwell House
(p. 231)

Repertory

Jonathan Fletcher
(p. 242)